NIMR

A Memoir of
Mischief and Mishap

Pter Newman Brooks

by
Peter Newman Brooks
Illustrated by Ian Levene

This memoir is largely fact, but part fiction. Real names have been
used except where that might cause embarrassment. Likewise,
most events and encounters took place as described. But the
reader will appreciate the problems that face an author seriously
attempting to fathom the feline mind.

Second Edition

First Published in 2007 by Milton Contact Ltd.
www.miltoncontact.com
in co-operation with *Moyhill* Publishing.

A CIP catalogue record for this book is available
from the British Library.

ISBN 978-1-905597-10-9

Cover portrait of Nimrod by Beverly Madley
Illustrations by Ian Levene

Typeset by *Moyhill* Publishing
Printed in UK

Moyhill Publishing,
Suite 471, 6 Slington House,
Rankine Rd., Basingstoke, RG24 8PH, UK.

Order online from *www.moyhill.com*

For RICHARD PETERS

Illustrations
Line drawings by Ian Levene

Photographs

Foreword

This little book tells the life story of a Siamese cat. Fact is often stranger than fiction and there's a bit of both here, for who can really penetrate the mind of a cat? The reader will certainly find it an unusual tale, focussed on a life crowded with incident. As the title indicates, here is a record of puss-cat mischief and mishap. So page by page, the life of an elegant creature is set out – a very full life played out in no fewer than four English counties as the cat moved about with those who cared for him.

In fact, Nimrod really had an extraordinary nine-life experience. For although there were the usual routines experienced by all pet lovers, many a crisis loomed to demand what are now called careful 'exit strategies'! When first spotted as a kitten, the puss captivated all with pure charm; and however frustrating those later acts of mischief – even of near madness in mishap! – Nimrod remained endearing to the end. He may not have merited a halo, but strained every sinew to surprise and be a shrewd Siamese of many parts. No wonder that all privileged to know him awarded the cat an aura of prestige.

Here too is an author's personal statement. For the memoir records a life-long love affair with cats – in particular, an abiding and deeply distilled fascination the writer felt for one truly remarkable Siamese.

P.N.B.

Prologue

Because of his fondness for felines, I, NIMROD, have allowed my Obliger, the author, to write this biography. My full life has certainly been demanding and left few spare moments for me to set about such a time-consuming task. In any case, writing about oneself can be boring, so the very thought of an autobiography I ruled out long ago. Yet when in repose, curled up with a paw over my eyes in many a favourite spot and summer sleeping place, I have often pondered the matter. And my considered opinion has brought me to a compromise I hope readers will find acceptable. Almost all my nine lives I have entrusted to my Obliger, and his very cattitude therefore makes him well qualified to write about them. But that will not prevent my including partial memoirs here and there, and these appear inset in the text set out in this special typeface with my monogram upon them.

1

NIMROD ENTERED PETER'S LIFE some time after his birth, but I have it on good authority that he and his siblings were born in the lower warming closet of a four-oven Aga cooker. He hailed from 'Old Oaks', Danbury, home of the Squire, his Lady and their daughter Anne; and that he was therefore an Essex cat may account for the star quality and staying power of his ever-purposeful presence on the planet.

Believe it or not, my mother was what Americans call a Calico cat!

Known as 'Turtle' to the human family at 'Old Oaks', that lady was tortoise-shell, and among others of course, must have fallen for a Siamese gentleman. To an essentially ginger puss, he was a fascinating fellow to meet; and letting known her availability, Turtle encouraged 'Chang' more than the many rivals ready and waiting to give her their undivided attention.

To keep tryst she found an ideal rendezvous in a large barn at the back of the house. Admittedly an old rooster and his flock had made their home there, but the odd charge and rally soon moved them on to clear the way for serious serenading. Generous coverings of hay and straw provided creature comfort at its very best; and making the most of her every opportunity, Turtle gave a whole range of male suitors the run around. Piteous pleading made clear that all were in with a chance, the lady being well aware that attention from various would-be fathers was by far the best way to guarantee posterity a colourful litter. For his part, 'Chang' gladly obliged, even escaping Turtle's wrath as he rose to leave. In truth she was glad to let him off, altogether delighted that a truly elegant gent had been prepared to give a mere tortoise-shell such fond attention. It certainly made her feel less of a hussy, however noisy their dating.

At kittening, the litter was large; and Turtle was delighted to find her first-born splendidly Siamese in colouring. From the start she noted his oriental paws, purring away with pride as she cleaned his miniature black pads. A testing moment for a first-time mother, she took her duties seriously, stimulating the lives of five further siblings as they arrived, licking away at pink paws and furry bodies with her raspy tongue. As diverse as their ancestry, the new arrivals proved a truly mixed bag. From the outset the second kitten was a shorthaired black, yet one discoloured by a mini-bib and white forepaw socks; and the third an orange tabby with a particularly bright necklaced chest. Anne, the daughter of the house and principal carer of Turtle, was to name them 'Bubbles and Squeak'. The fourth kitten was another red, but so blotched about with white as to afford him a rustic look duly meriting the name 'Roger'. And finally, five and six, a boy and the only little girl, were tabbies of strikingly similar mix. Their dark brown, grey and white coats were difficult to distinguish; and granted the comical but endearing behaviour they would later display, Anne's mother suggested 'Ernie' and 'Erica' for names.

A London attorney, the Squire of 'Old Oaks' tolerated his daughter's pet cats but left their care to her; and she, as often as not, to her mother. This proved no easy task when 'Brandy', Turtle's sister, had herself been delivered of a litter only weeks before. Complaining of a 'catty chaos' and of 'too much fur underfoot', the Squire made dreadful threats, on more than one occasion suggesting dire solutions to what was fast becoming a population problem. In fact it seemed that his sole interest lay in condemning the cats and calling them names. 'Yah', 'Booh', he would exclaim when their paths crossed; and if they did not, he even went out of his way to pounce on the diminutive unwary kittens. Yet when good-humoured after dinner – by then often in his cups – expletives were abandoned and a prophetic role assumed. Such a mood once prompted him to transform Roger the Rustic into 'Hodge' – 'Hodge' the erstwhile furry foil of the learned Doctor Samuel Johnson. Equally, a mean mood could still prompt the man to wrath, cats and kittens alike fleeing from his very presence even if not actually pursued. 'Nimrod' he neither named nor liked, merely referring to 'that Yowler' as 'Waah', a scurrilous misnomer the 'Old Oaks' family observed as 'Miaow', 'Meoouw' or plan 'Mio' for short.

Needless to state, neither Turtle nor Brandy approved of such a casual attitude to their progeny, both mothers pursuing a policy of splendid isolation by regularly removing little ones well out of range. In early days, carried by the scruff of the neck, kittens were conveyed upstairs to bedrooms; hidden away behind cushions in the drawing room; and occasionally taken down the cellar steps to adorn a comfortable tinderbox by the entrance. Once weaned of course, there were excursions into the garden, and even to the hallowed barnyard domain revered by their mothers as 'Lovers' Lane'.

There were days when temporary solutions of this kind successfully hid kittens away. For the Squire followed regular routines. At home in his work room he pored over law reports preparing cases for clients; and away in London, Court life kept him far from all cats. Once back from the big city, however, particularly when he chose to patrol beyond the confines of a study shrewdly observed by Turtle, Brandy and all kittens to be way out of bounds, he found his beloved 'Old Oaks' under territorial threat. It had become a *catscape.* Wherever you looked there were cats: common black cats; terrible tabbies; gingers; a tortoise-shell cat; and now even a rowdy, half-caste Siamese! To relax indoors was no easy matter. Few chairs were unoccupied; in the library, bookcases provided popular draught-free niches; and in the kitchen, bar stools stood tall as pedestals for cats. When bedroom doors were left ajar too, retiring could be fraught for those without spectacles, scatter cushions and even pillows turning into curled-up, snoozing cats. Even the garden – prized by villagers and widely known in the region for its colourful beds and magnificent border display – had begun to resemble a battlefield. For kittens have to be taught to dig, and once trained by their mothers, eagerly did so all over the place as if the annual autumn planting of bulbs must now be a daily occurrence.

No small wonder then that when daughter Anne returned from Dorset – home for the Easter holiday with a school friend she had invited to stay – her father gave notice of a 'round-table conference'. He announced no agenda; and tired from their journey the girls took tea before Jenny was shown to her guest room. Once unpacked, there was the house to see, a fine eighteenth-century property with outbuildings set in several acres of garden, meadow and woodland. Revisiting her old haunts delighted Anne; and Jenny enjoyed the sheer scale of her best friend's rambling retreat. There was a swimming pool; tennis courts too; and what promise these held for the holiday.

It had been a long, busy Term, and the girls were glad to sit and gossip on the terrace. The peace of the country-side, and warm sunshine in the late afternoon provided the perfect context for the arrival of Turtle. Emerging from the house through the French window in the drawing room, she came to renew her bond with Anne; and Jenny observed her gliding along with raised tail. But barely had the mother cat sniffed to say 'Hello' when her brood rushed on parade. Overjoyed, and completely captivated by the kittens, the girls spent the next hour cuddling and playing with a ragbag of mischief, their proud, purring parent keeping a watchful eye as they did so.

A more distant onlooker, the Squire observed the scene from the study window, and later, at dinner, chose to com-ment. He had prepared his case well. A serious population problem had to be faced. Anne's absence demanded a review of her pets. Now that both Brandy and Turtle had experienced motherhood, a visit to the Vet was essential if the house was not to be overrun with cats. Neither he nor Anne's mother could continue to take full responsibility for her animals; and Anne had herself reached an age when she simply had to realize that the world contained far too many furry frivolities.

As if to punctuate the point her father was making, there was a sudden rush of scuttling paws as Erica and Ernie raced into the dining room dribbling a little wedge of folded silver paper under the table, with Bubbles, Squeak and Roger in hot pursuit. The Squire was quick to react: banging the board, the flat of his hand achieved a resonance that almost spilt his wine, as the terrified kittens fled back to the kitchen.

"See what I mean!" he snorted. "We simply must make plans … find homes … or ourselves move out!"

"Don't be so dramatic, dear." It was Anne's mother's turn to speak. "I'm sure the girls will find a solution. Remember our daughter hopes to be a Vet one day; and to square up to this little matter will surely give her useful experience?"

Jenny was perplexed, if not bewildered; Anne depressed; and a temporary silence descended before the conversation changed, this time to focus on the past Term's activity, and the high and low periods the girls had endured at School. Both sport and study came under scrutiny; and Anne and Jenny announced that, in their view at least, the House, and even the Head Mistress, were sending good progress reports.

Despite a welcome return to home cooking, it had been an embarrassing meal and the girls were glad to escape to Anne's room after dinner. There they pondered what was clearly a serious matter, and putting their heads together, they tried to think of a solution that would secure a satisfactory future for the kittens. Anne was eager for her best friend to adopt a puss. But in Jenny's view, her parents, Peter and Grace, were dog, not cat, people, so there seemed little chance of success there. Just imagine the predicament of a kitten obliged to face a 'Wow-Wow'! The very thought of it could only extend the crisis. Nevertheless, there must surely be folk who could fall for such adorable pets, and the girls agreed on action to seek them out. So together they made a list of friends and neighbours who must surely need one, if not two or three, cats.

A careful survey was thus drawn up, and from memory Anne beat the bounds of her parish introducing Jenny to local characters as she did so. There was, for example, old Rose Tye, a widow whose aged 'Kit Kat' had just succumbed to endless sleep after years of overindulgence. Evidently a 'live-to-eat' cat, and quite distinct from those simple-minded mousers satisfied with an 'eat-to-live' agenda, Kit Kat's vast presence had earned him the soubriquet 'Greedy-Guts'. And as he ballooned over the years, old 'Greedy-Guts' became something of a myth in his own lifetime. Surely he could now be replaced with an affectionate kitten, and Mrs Tye invited to make her selection from the Brandy-Turtle progeny? Then too, there was the Bebbington family: they had no cats. Admittedly Anne seemed to recall their interest in birds. They had an aviary after all; and dogs guarded their extraordinary property. *Dogs*! That word prompted Jenny's intervention. Her pet was a Corgi, but 'Jane' could never be classed as a 'guard dog'!

"Well, if you had the strange collection of outhouses the Bebbingtons class as home," Anne interjected, "you too would need patrols from roving Rotweilers!"

Next for consideration was the Parish Priest whose vast Vicarage must surely offer real potential for something of a 'Pets' Corner'? The house in question almost paralleled 'Old Oaks' in size, and could clearly accommodate at least two evacuees. Yet to approach Father Thackray was a risky business for, should the 'one-good-turn-deserves-another' principle be observed, regular church-going might have to follow, and that was a risk Anne did not wish to take. In any case, there were ten (or was it actually *eleven?*) kittens to contend with; and at this rate the girls had to admit defeat. The hamlet of Danbury was simply inadequate.

Saddened by her friend's evident concern and subsequent frustration, Jenny began to wonder if her home neighbours might prove a better bet. But it did not take long for her just as readily to dismiss the idea. For when at home, she lived in a Cathedral Close where life tended to be far too regulated for displaced felines. Never a girl to give up, however, and fully determined to help Anne, she suggested publicity. Could they not attract the attention of passers-by with an eye-catching notice? Then too, with the comparative freedom a school holiday provided, might they not interview inquirers to make sure that good homes were on offer? Anne was enthusiastic, and together they planned posters and a homemade leaflet raid. They would put up a notice on the board at *The Village Stores*, and even spend pocket money advertising in the local paper.

Next morning after breakfast the girls busied themselves with just such a task, and did so with purposeful intent. Unquestioning, Anne's parents wondered what was afoot; but with last evening's scene still simmering, chose not to interfere. The girls seemed content enough in the playroom; and daily routines forged ahead. By lunch time the sound of hammering from an outhouse partly explained two late arrivals at table; but still no questions were asked. After all, "I hope you've washed?" was as recurrent a question before meals as the "Of course, Mummy!" reply. So lunch proceeded at speed, an unusual silence only heightening adult suspicions. Clearly something was up, but in strained circumstances it seemed wise to wait on events and ask no questions.

By mid-afternoon two resolute figures were observed going down the front drive towards the road. One carried a large board fixed to a stake, the other a club hammer.

❦

Jenny's parents could not wait to welcome their daughter home again. They had chosen to send her to school in Dorset because the distance of that county from Kent made boarding a reality and no weekly compromise. If Peter and Grace did not stint their visits to Sherborne, by avoiding weekly trips in Term, they not only helped their daughter's House Mistress in her pledge to make girls' free time 'activity full', but also ensured that holiday home times were highly prized. So when the first weekend of Spring Break was to be spent with Anne in Essex, and Jenny's return a little delayed, their only daughter was the more eagerly awaited. And determined to make the most of Easter as a family, Peter and Grace drove across to Danbury to make the final leg of her homeward journey easier for Jenny.

Peter and Grace had not previously been to Danbury

and were uncertain of the way. After negotiating the traffic chaos of Chelmsford, they almost lost themselves in the leafy lanes of rural Essex. Advised over the telephone that Anne's parents lived in 'a lovely period house well off the road', their approach was slow and studied lest they miss the driveway. In one respect they need not have worried, most houses displaying signs on the roadside verge. As Peter drove along the twisty lane with due care and attention, Grace read these out:

"'Barn Owls'; 'The Mill'; and the ever-deadly 'Dun Roamin,'" she droned.

"'The Old Rectory'; 'Bluebells'; and 'Punch Farm'", as they crawled along.

"Nothing here," she announced as the road ahead meandered through a colourful tree tunnel towards another bend. But then, quite suddenly, a large placard came into view carrying what looked like a slogan.

'KITTENS FREE TO GOOD HOMES', it read, and was clearly the work of amateurs. Suggesting he bring the barouche to a halt, Grace told Peter she guessed the notice to be the handiwork of enterprising youngsters – even children inspired by those BBC 'Blue Peter' Presenters? Whatever the truth of the matter, they were wise to stop, for the sheer size of the notice completely obscured any motorist's eye view of the sign for 'Old Oaks'. Fortunately for them that was not the case, and although the angle turn was decidedly sharp, they didn't overshoot and managed to steer the car into a long shady drive. Finding their way through a little copse, they were

soon in open country again, and there beheld what was surely a stately home.

"Impressive house, my dear," said Peter to his wife.

"It is indeed – I do hope I'm properly dressed for such society," came her nervous response.

"Don't you worry about that? Just look at me!"

The car parked, and the bell rung, they duly awaited response half hoping their daughter and her friend would answer. There seemed instead to be no reply, and Peter rang again, this time loud and long. Eventually it was the Squire himself who obliged with a bored "Yes? Can I help you?"

"We've come to collect our daughter…" Grace paused.

"Oh … of course … [and grudgingly]… You'd better come in."

Tired after their trip, and somewhat crestfallen by the lack of any real welcome, Jenny's parents entered the hallway fearful lest their daughter had been an unwelcome burden to her host.

"I don't know where the girls have gone…" mumbled the Squire, "but do wait here."

Surveying the scene in semi-silence, the newcomers seemed more appealing to a fine marmalade cat than to the Squire. For in repose from a comfortable chair, 'Brandy' uttered a 'chirrup' of recognition and, when stroked by Grace, began to purr loudly.

"A curious welcome," Peter commented, "but at least one member of the household seems pleased to greet us! Where are those girls?"

"Patience dear; they cannot be far away, and perhaps their absence is a game?" She continued to caress the cat and then added, trying hard to encourage a measure of patience in her spouse: "You know what youngsters are like!"

After what seemed an age, it was the Squire who reappeared. Still in nonchalant mood, he declined to utter a word, and indifference reigned until, framed in a far doorway, a troupe of kittens raced into the hall. Then it was Peter who took the initiative: "My word," he exclaimed with a laugh. "What a motley menagerie! No wonder they're being offered 'FREE TO GOOD HOMES'!"

Embarrassed, Grace rapidly made reference to the notice at the end of the drive.

Clearly unaware of this, and temporarily confused,

the Squire inquired further. But as he did so a pert little Siamese kitten appeared and, lit up by a shaft of sunlight, did so to advantage. Full of admiration, it was then Peter's turn to comment.

"Now Sir, if that cat is included in the offer … We would be interested!"

It proved a precious moment for, descending the stairs, Jenny had heard her father's offer. Running down to greet her parents, she jumped for joy, embraced Anne, and let everyone know how much she had always wanted a kitten.

"Well you're certainly welcome to young 'Yowla'," Anne's father responded. "One down, and ten to go!" he calculated, and instructing his daughter to find a travelling basket, the Squire bade Jenny farewell, nodded to her parents, and withdrew.

"Is the kitten really called 'Yowla'?" Grace inquired.

"Not really," said Anne. "My father is such a tease with cats, and as far as he has noticed this particular kitten at all, it was to call him 'Meoow', or was it 'Mio'? I think mummy knows more, but she's out until seven."

With that Anne went to find the basket, and while Jenny gathered her luggage together, Peter loaded up the car. It was with a moist eye that Anne took leave of her friend, and patted the kitten. Placing him gently into the gloomy basket too, she held 'Mio' aloft before the scrum of assembled siblings. "Say bye bye," she half sobbed, Aunt Brandy looking on in amazement.

With his Mother Turtle still absent, it was with a heavy heart and pitiful mew that the little fellow clawed at the wickerwork while the basket lid was fastened. For departure, and a move into the unknown effectively brought life as he had known it to an end. His short spell of early kittenhood at 'Old Oaks' was apparently over, and in transit he felt sadly stressed. His familiar surroundings had disappeared, and with them his sense of security. For no brief glance at his school of siblings was enough to dispel his depression as he mourned their loss. Even if this new family of humans – Peter, Grace and Jenny – proved kindness itself, he had lost his mother, and nothing would ever be the same again.

After reading these lines and looking back on my infancy, I should add that I don't recall much. Nevertheless I am prepared to add my impurrmatur.

2

The kitten's confinement in that travelling basket did not please him at all. Such a prison proved claustrophobic even to a small ball of Siamese fur. Most of Jenny's luggage – a large school trunk, her valise, violin case, toilet and shoe bags, together with a curiously curved wooden pole he later learnt to identify as a 'hockey stick' – was locked away in a black hole at the back of the car. Somehow it seemed to be outside; and inside the human family were able to sit down as they went on their way. His own place was on the back seat where, in the basket, he found himself next to Jenny. From time to time she poked a finger through the wicker trying to reassure her new pet. At first, responding with a 'chirrup', he did his best to return the greeting; but with no room to manoeuvre, let alone massage his chin, Mio deemed it best to doze the journey away. In any case the noise of the machine, not to mention many judders and bumps from uneven roads, made beauty sleep out of the question. So to catnap seemed the wisest way to face this first test of endurance.

When comparative calm returned, he felt himself airlifted into new surroundings. The lid of the basket was raised, and there, surrounding him on all sides, his new family knelt on the tiled floor of what was clearly a kitchen.

"Poor little orphan." It was Peter who spoke, Jenny and Grace in support raising the kitten on high before he was lowered to face a saucer of freshly-poured milk. A kind thought to be sure, for the ordeal had made him thirsty. But this was no moment either to drink or, much less, to settle down; and coming to the rescue at once, kitten instinct insisted on a security test. Anything might happen to take such a youngster unawares; and was there not a pervasive smell of DOG? So without delay Mio set about seeking any sanctuary that could keep him out of harm's way in an emergency.

At a glance he noted a high-level windowsill. This was well within range, and could surely be reached in three bounds: floor to stool; stool to table; and table to sill. And skilfully avoiding a crowded vase of flowers, a four-point landing was satisfactorily achieved without even the use of braking claws. The view was superb, and to the family's surprise their kitten, once perched on this eminence, serenely surveyed the scene both inside and out. Then, with a triumphant expression on his black face, Mio began to purr.

Framed against the window beside the pink tulips, his pose provided the perfect portrait of a young Siamese. What an impact he made too, Peter, Grace and Jenny reacting in their various ways as the kitten cast his spell. For Peter his little head could have been carved out of ebony, the very silhouette of such a tiny black nose giving Mio a truly aristocratic appearance. In her turn, Grace found the little fellow's colouring fascinating. Even at this early stage before the various hues had begun to darken in tone, the contrast between his pale cream body, dark chocolate feet and elegant whip tail proved impressive. And on Jenny, his periwinkle-blue eyes – already showing that slight, even mischievous, squint of the Siamese – had a hypnotic effect.

From the eyrie soft purring continued, the contented murmuring of acceptance. Clearly pleased that he had gained the family's undivided attention, the kitten seemed glad of a new home. Thankful to be taken in, he now felt it safe to stay, and warbled permission to be fed.

≈≈

The days that followed were full of activity and interest as Mio settled in to his Canterbury home. Soon aware that he had much to say, the family, trying hard to understand his every request, rapidly realized why the kitten had been known as 'Yowla' to the Squire of Danbury. For though very much the midget, Mio was in no way mute but rather the possessor of a full-throated voice. This he used to greet and meet; to seek attention; to demand entrance or exit; to express satisfaction and to swear displeasure.

Jenny had experienced the full force of 'hissing' almost as soon as the kitten took up residence. With her parents occupied elsewhere in the house, she had decided to introduce Mio to her other pet, a much-loved Corgi called 'Jane'. After the return trip from Essex, it was sensible to keep the pets apart, at least for a few hours. So Jane was confined to a utility room to ensure peace for the new arrival in the kitchen. Only a door apart, each animal was nevertheless well aware of the other's presence; and the wooden boundary between them regularly subjected to sniffles and snuffles of every kind. But then, while Peter parked the car, and Grace was upstairs unpacking the contents of the school trunk ready for washday, Jenny took the initiative and, kitten in hand, opened the door.

Chaos immediately resulted: Jane's displeasure was instantaneous! Madly barking, the Corgi jumped and snapped at an unwelcome intruder who clearly threatened the home! Yet the hysterical noise made by the dog paled into insignificance before the deep-throated oaths and vicious hissing that came from the kitten! Altogether shattered by such over-reaction, but with due presence of mind, Jenny held the kitten tight. Reaching out too she just managed to return Mio to the windowsill retreat he had so recently discovered. And there he continued to hiss and swear while, below, the bewildered Corgi did her best to reach out to him, her forepaws tearing away at a kitchen stool. Hearing the hubbub, Peter and Grace returned to do what they could to calm the situation. Their full range of soothing words seemed to register well enough, and, reassured, the pets calmed down.

It was now imperative that both animals became aware that they were highly prized. Equally, domestic matters had to take their normal course and do so without too much interference. So although the human family made sure that at least one guardian stayed in the kitchen, Jane and Mio were given space to get to know each other at close quarters. In this way hostility gradually receded. A lengthy period of armed neutrality followed, and this was played out on different levels. Above sat the cat; below paced the dog. For initially Mio simply stayed aloft on the sill. Jane meanwhile toured the tiles where, ever the glutton, she also lapped up what little milk remained in the kitten's saucer. Next, making a partial descent, Mio chose to walk along table tops, prowling with agitated tail past pots on cupboard working surfaces. By this time it was a bored Corgi who retired to her bed; and there, in customary comfort, nose on cushion but with foxy ears alert, Jane silently scrutinised the Siamese interloper. Barely an hour ago she had been terrorized by the snarls of a hissing foe; now more accurate focus not only revealed an innocent, but also aroused maternal feelings that must surely accept, if not adopt, this orphan kitten. Before long too, Mio was back on *terra firma*. Inspecting all corners of the room, he circled the dog's bed, even pausing to sniff her very person. Evidently appreciated, the gesture was returned and, to the amazement of three human spectators, Corgi and kitten settled in together, the best of friends!

The high drama of first meeting a Corgi is one of my most vivid memories. But I think I should qualify this reference by my being 'the best of friends' with any canine! Admittedly dogs do have their place; but when I chose to sleep in Jane's bed, my Obliger had still to find me a place of my own. So accuracy demands the reader should realize that I was converted more by comfort than by love of any dog. Equally, the proximity of such a retreat to the warmth of the Aga must be taken into account!

❦

Now in Canterbury, Mio's continuing kittenhood was largely confined to the Close. For Peter, his principal Obliger, taught at the school and, as Precentor, directed services in the great cathedral church there. The massive stone structure quite dwarfed the family's little house even as it also dominated Anselm Hall next door where lived a Canon Craddock.

An elderly, most genial, priest, Craddock was devoted to cats, three of whom gazed at Mio when the kitten began to explore the garden. Inside the Hall they stared out; and conscious that six eyes studied his every movement, he trusted he was not the cause of any offence. Mouthing many a mew, the kitten felt sure of attention; but that was not to come before the Reverend Canon had himself sent a Vet round to greet and meet him. It seemed that Craddock's aged cat – 'Ginger is *ninety*' the Canon proudly confided to all who met his puss – was somewhat 'out of salts' and in need of professional attention. Ever protective of his cats too, Craddock knew that any new arrival needed a thorough check-up. It was consideration that saved a visit to the surgery – and a very kind thought for a kitten well able to recall that nasty spell of confinement in a travelling basket. So after examining 'Ginger', Mr Blount called round to attend on Mio.

A man of few words (Blount by name and blunt by nature in fact), the Vet was well enough versed in felines. First he chose to comment on his furry little patient's status, and did so in forthright terms.

"No pedigree this," he chortled, "but good enough as a Siamese look-alike!" And then in brief elaboration: "Pale enough now … but he'll turn *brown* later!"

Heeding such pronouncements, Peter confirmed the kitten's origin as far as he could, and added that family priority sought health before value. He wanted a pet "sound in wind and limb," a cat "in the pink of condition, not fur," a feline so physically fit he could enjoy a long life and value the care and comfort of a good family home!

"Glad to hear it," came Blount's reply, very much a regular no-nonsense refrain used on new clients. Setting the little creature at ease, the Vet held the kitten with a firm hand while skilfully probing its vital organs. And all was carried out in a manner so effective that the survey seemed no more than tender fondling. Encouraged rather than embarrassed, Mio was at peace with himself and began to purr. A vigorous jerk followed, a tail pull the kitten appeared to favour as a new kind of experience. At once the Vet spoke with a statement of the obvious, for turning to Peter he announced, "You have a boy!" Then, strangely, and *sotto voce*, "I'll need to see him again in a month or so." Without a pause, Blount flashed a light in the kitten's eyes, explored his ears, and as purr turned to snarl, and snarl to gargle, the Vet examined Mio's throat.

"What do you know about cats?" he inquired.

"Little enough," Peter replied. "This is my first. But we have a dog."

Blount laughed, and Mio, with an old-fashioned look in one so young, seemed to take offence.

"Cats are rarely ill," the Vet continued, "but beware of feline *enteritis*. Bring him for injection." And a number of rambling comments concluded the interview.

"If your puss scratches, don't worry. So do you! It is not *enteritis.* That you'll know well enough when he's really off his food … Mmm … I'll give you a diet sheet … But when he lies on cold tiles … even over his water bowl, yet won't drink, he could be in danger. So if that ever happens, get on the 'phone at once. The virus in question is highly infectious, so don't come to the surgery, for any contact would endanger my other patients."

And popping a pellet in Mio's mouth, Blount turned to go. "They all have worms, you know; but this chap's in robust, even rude, health. Keep him that way!"

As soon as the Vet left, the kitten began furiously to wash; and this time it was no mere sporadic undertaking, but a detailed ablution ceremony as, with far more care than usual, the little fellow turned from a preliminary scratch to run through a full grooming session of fur coat, all four paws and underclothes. As he reached his tail too, he seemed strangely stressed, but once petted and reassured, began to purr aloud, his tiny barbed tongue returning the compliment by licking Peter's hand.

My encounter with the Vet – now but a distant memory – was most embarrassing. I may have been fondled, but he did so presume. Perhaps his manner was meant to tell me that even a youngster had friends in high places? After all, the sudden appearance of a stranger who only came to give me his undivided attention, and then left without further ado was surely unusual? If he said very little, and almost nothing to me, I could tell that he cared for my kind. For did I not spot a sample of colourful cat hairs on his tweeds? And together with that swatch, did I not catch the scent of someone experienced, someone who knew about puss-cat life and death? So despite a natural anxiety, I felt I could trust him.

⚮

Towering above the city rooftops, and dominating the green courts and gardens that enclosed his new home, the great cathedral overshadowed the kitten's Canterbury years. Bemused and inclined to compete when bells tolled, he was fascinated by the moving mass of pilgrims to the Precincts. He had clearly come to live in a very special place. No longer the rural calm of Essex, but a heaving hubbub of visitors. Although most were impressed with the architectural splendour of their surroundings, many found a fascinating distraction in the kitten as he gazed down at them from the top of the garden wall. Truly, these were

busy times, and although days sped by almost as fast as the Jackdaws circling the cathedral towers, several exploits from the tender youth of kittenhood cannot be ignored.

First, a developing friendship with Jane introduced the kitten to a dog's life; and the Corgi soon proved herself a real pal. The golden rule was to keep your distance at meal times: once observe that custom and a cat could rest assured that his presence was welcome. So when Mio fancied a game, Jane readily obliged; and in no time at all, the two enjoyed regular rough and tumbles together. Indoors these disturbed the peace and often damaged the furniture. When the animals managed to invade the hall, 'stair-racing' was a favourite pastime. A kind of steeplechase, the diversion involved Corgi chasing cat on high, cat in turn repelling the advance with a downstairs sortie. From the landing windowsill too, the kitten could swing his tail and keep it just out of range, the black-furred pendulum further provoking his playmate in the process. The result proved so rowdy that quieter mortals found outside activity preferable, and the terrible two were soon shown the back door. In turn, this expulsion from the house led to the foundation of a firm of 'Garden Wreckers'.

Peter made quite a hobby of horticulture, and had a passion for climbing plants. They gave colour and a kind of architectural interest to a small garden. They also prompted him to erect a rustic archway and adjoining trellis; and this served to support several fine and expensive specimens he and his wife planted and tied to the framework. It was a project that mystified Jane and Mio who carefully observed the workers from the terrace. The kitten in particular was keen to help; so he did what he could to pounce on the garden twine (or was it the tail of a mouse?), and unwind rather more than was required for knotting. And then, when the gardeners retired for refreshment, the 'wreckers' took over!

Clear that he could climb far higher than any clematis, Mio clawed his way to the top of the trellis, Jane at his heels yapping her encouragement. No autumn gale could have been more effective in blowing down the vine, a plant simultaneously shredded by the constant treadmill of Corgi forefeet. By this time, the rustic arch boasted a fur finial, a catchy cry from the high-flown kitten further frustrating Jane as she blustered beneath. What a sight to confront Peter and Grace after coffee! The gardeners found themselves face-to-face with 'Garden Wreckers'; for pets had become pests to present yet another challenge to the otherwise restful pursuit and charm of horticulture.

≈≈

The next episode of life in Canterbury also cast Corgis, this time giving Jane a centre-stage role. In terms of Mio's biography the matter may seem misplaced, but in view of the growing friendship between the two animals is hardly irrelevant. Newsworthy too, it embraced a 'happy event' that merits the most honourable mention. Briefly, before the kitten had even come to live in Canterbury, through the good offices of a Mrs Lepper of Wye, Jane had been introduced to a most attentive gentleman, Pembroke by pedigree. They got on well, and although she was no longer in touch, their brief encounter proved productive in every way. For the milk of canine kindness that had so recently pitied a furry orphan was now to flow in reality and feed a fine brood of pups. But let the *Kentish Gazette* report [6 August, 1971] with its front-page headline:

JANE'S BUMPER BUNDLE

'When Patch, the popular doggy pal of BBC TV's "Blue Peter" died earlier this year, hundreds of children mourned his passing.

But in [a Canterbury household] Jenny gazed at her pregnant Corgi, Jane, and put her generous mind to work.

She thought if Jane was going to produce offspring, and she very clearly was, then Blue Peter might as well have one of the pups as a replacement for Patch.

She wrote to the BBC with her offer but was given a kindly cold nose… "The programme was extremely grateful for her offer" [wrote the Editor] "but felt unable at the time to accept another puppy."

So the great day arrived – and it was not the usual four or five pups that Corgis usually produce, but a handsome litter of seven – almost enough to stock the Queen's kennels.

Now Jane's family, nicknamed "The People" by Jenny's father… is almost as uncontrollable as Canterbury shoppers on a Saturday morning.

Penned up where proud mother Jane can keep a watchful eye on them, her first litter waste away their daylight hours eating, drinking and sunning them-

Jane's bumper bundle

When Patch, the popular doggy pal of B.B.C. Television's Blue Peter programme died earlier this year, hundreds of children mourned his passing.

But in [a Canterbury household] 10-year-old Jenny Brooks gazed at her pregnant Corgi, Jane, and put her generous mind to work.

She thought if Jane was going to produce offspring, and she very clearly was, then Blue Peter might as well have one of the pups as a replacement for Patch.

She wrote to the B.B.C. with her offer but was given a kindly cold nose by Biddy Baxter, Blue Peter's Editor.

The programme, wrote Miss Baxter, was extremely grateful for her offer but felt unable at the time to accept another puppy.

So the great day arrived—and it was the not usual four or five pups that Corgi usually produce, but a handsome litter of seven —almost enough to stock the Queen's kennels.

Now Jane's family, nicknamed "The People" by Jenny's

father, Dr Peter Brooks, is six weeks old and almost as uncontrollable as Canterbury shoppers on a Saturday morning.

Penned-up where proud mother Jane can keep a watchful eye on them, her first litter waste away their daylight hours eating, drinking and sunning themselves in true Cricket Week tradition. At night they are put out of harm's way in the garage.

To give this shaggy dog story a happy, if not a funny, ending, Jenny says the offer to the B.B.C. is still open.

selves in true Cricket Week tradition. At night they are kept out of harm's way…

To give this shaggy dog story a happy, if not funny, ending, Jenny says the offer to the BBC is still open.

Enough said: I really must add a careful cat corrective to this partial account from the press. It makes no mention of me, and readers need to know that the single-minded, attentive gaze of a Siamese more than parallels the 'watchful eye' of any mother Corgi! Media photos are all very well; but for those who can count, only six pups appear in the picture the paper printed. The photographer has left out Bess, the little tricolour later to become my best friend. And that is unforgivable.

On the subject of dogs too, Mio left his biographer to relate a startling instalment of high drama. Kindly heed his own introduction to the narrative:

I'm told that humans have a proverb, 'Let sleeping dogs lie'; and an early memory has to be recorded when I suffered for doing just that! I'll allow my Obliger to tell the tale, and myself simply state that, free to roam without Corgi distraction and active canine support, I faced the worst crisis of my kittenhood in those far-off Canterbury days.

No doubt the Corgi reference is used to seek sympathy for what, on his part, was not so much juvenile error as inexcusable misjudgement. Yet in his defence readers ought to recall the sadness of early separation from his mother, a premature parting that deprived the kitten of much basic training. Bravado is all very well, but it can easily lead to disaster. So much this account will indicate.

Jane's puppies demanded the fullest attention all day long, and if Peter, Grace and Jenny duly observed a duty roster to feed and keep 'The People' clean and safe, the kitten assumed his own responsibilities as a playmate-observer. What larks they had, bounding and chasing, rolling and tumbling up and over on the lawn, enclosed in their wired run. Outside the mesh Mio kept vigil ever alert for the great escape. The slightest interest secured immediate puppy response; and the very sight and scent of a patrolling kitten – in age almost a recruit for the people pack – guaranteed ecstatic clamour from the litter. When present herself, mother Jane lay back to feed the frenzy, her milk bar ever ready to refresh the weary. And from dawn to dusk kitten provoked and pups pursued until exhaustion bade them beat retreat and lie to sleep.

As 'The People' bedded down one fine night, Mio became aware of rustling in the straw. Did not something move in an otherwise still and silent run? And was not that a different kind of tail in view? Sharp-eyed and prick-eared in an instant, the kitten found himself on edge, transfixed by the sight of a hairy brown foe. The creature's beady eyes, waggling whiskers and cunning grin made him freeze; and with arched back and raised fur mane enhancing his size, his tail flailed with fury. However uninstructed, instinct informed him that here was a Brown Rat, a cat's traditional foe, an enemy deserving no quarter.

If the rodent paused awhile, it did not linger in the pen and soon scuttled off into the night. In hot pursuit Mio – now not so much a kitten and more an adolescent feeling his claws – followed, and the obstacle race was on. Leading to the Precincts, the garden gate slowed the kitten down. Vermin could squeeze beneath: a cat must vault. But from his vantage point on top of the gate, Mio viewed the course taken by his quarry. Evidently following an evening routine, the rat ran parallel to the great Gothic cathedral using litterbins as staging posts. Placed at regular intervals for the use of tidy tourists, these provided him and his kind with any morsels disdained by pigeons (and, from time to time, even feral felines). When the rat slowed to forage too, the kitten closed the gap; but whenever Mio made ready to pounce, the rodent scampered on, making for the next bin. Such a chase continued until, dwarfed by the Christchurch

Gateway, the rat reached the final receptacle the Precincts had to offer, an overflowing bin yielding irresistible culinary delights. Brought to a halt by such bounty, it was ready to dine; and the kitten, now well within range, prepared to make that final stoop to savour a kill of his own. Yet it was not to be as, all of a sudden, both rat and cat endured the full footlight experience of actors on stage at a moment of high drama. For they had been exposed by glaring headlights, the lights of a car trundling across the cobbled entrance to the Precincts. Disturbed, the animals fled, cat chasing rat through the medieval gateway into the busy network of streets in the city centre beyond.

Now aware that it was at risk too, the rat raced home. Entering Palace Street, it made for its nearest lair, and sped into the basement of an antique gallery. Undaunted, the incautious kitten was close behind; and at a mad pace for small pads, manoeuvred a metal grill to gain access to the cellar through an open window the bars concealed. Although well able to fall on his feet, Mio found himself winded by the drop. Worse though was the frustration he felt: he had lost his prey; the rat had already gone to ground; and he was imprisoned.

Initially, the fact that he was also lost and away from his own home did not worry the kitten. He had been thwarted, and turned to trim his claws on a conveniently upholstered chair. Then it was time to spray, and at least remind the rat that he could challenge the rights of any rodent. But what then? Perhaps a grooming session? He certainly felt unclean; and in the absence of an Obliger who could always be relied on to pet and stroke away anxieties, had to console himself.

So, from the seat of a padded sofa, Mio surveyed his surroundings. In half light poorly reflected from lamp posts
in the street outside, it seemed a curious scene. The walls
were hung with pictures; the floor piled high with furniture;
and even the ceiling well nigh dangled with chandeliers
and pendant unlit fittings. At the rear a large double door
was firmly fastened; and the only other exit appeared to be
a window. This was of course the window through which
he had fallen when chasing the rat. Mounted high up the
wall facing Palace Street, it may have provided emergency

access, but by design offered no point of departure. *Hopper-hung* and meant solely for ventilation, it was appropriate in a storeroom. Below the floorboards too, the rodent world had no complaints, self-sufficient rat-runs offering every facility for exit in a maze of underground galleries. For a cat matters were very different. The routine of an active life demanded sleep and exploration; sleep and grooming; more sleep and a forage. But forage without return, without food or water, could not last long.

It was thus a bewildered kitten that found respite in slumber land. He slept soundly too, so soundly in fact that when he awoke the morning was already far advanced. A brilliant sun shone into the basement, and although last evening's depressing gloom had departed, daylight confirmed the impossibility of any escape from his confinement. Impatient at such a predicament, Mio paced to and fro like a caged tiger. With hurried pads he went, but all to no avail. One last resort remained, and that a truly Siamese stratagem: in his quandary he would go vocal! Friday was a busy shopping day, and yowling might just draw attention from passers-by, all of whom needed to know of a puss cat's plight and of the tight corner in which he found himself.

❦

For Peter, the prospect of a peaceful Thursday evening was soon to turn into a nightmare. With his wife away visiting Jenny for the weekend, he fancied a musical interlude as an antidote to the kennel-maid duties imposed by 'The People'. But with Mio missing, any such plan was out of the question and a full-scale search soon set in train. In

Canon Craddock's experience, missing cats were either road victims or 'shut ins'. Only rarely were they stolen, even though Burmese, Siamese and Persian kittens tended to be most at risk. Calming Peter's panic, the old gentleman promised to make special arrangements before cathedral services if the kitten had not shown up by Sunday. And for his part Peter soon persuaded selected senior boys from the school to help search the Precincts. In the dark this was no easy task, all too many green courts, cloistered walks, gardens and walled alleys offering sanctuary for a lonesome fur waif. And if the little Siamese had chanced to enter the great cathedral church itself, however confused he would at least be safe for the night.

Friday morning came, and when boys attending Matins had nothing to report, Peter suggested publicity. Notices appealing for information were hastily composed, and these volunteers fly-posted in the Precincts. Such eager beavers likewise circulated details to a range of premises in neighbouring streets where the kitten could have strayed.

LOST

A young Siamese cat (male)
strayed from the Cathedral Precincts
on Thursday evening.
Any sighting, or other information, please
report to the Verger at the West Porch,
Or telephone the Precentor

REWARD.

Saturday came, and still no news. But with Craddock on duty as Canon in Residence, the promised appeal to congregations was made early, and at Evensong, elegantly phrased like a lesser Litany, a notice made all aware of the absent kitten.

Throughout Sunday too, the announcement rang forth albeit to no avail. So when Monday dawned, it was a faint-hearted Peter who telephoned the Council Offices to inquire if the Canterbury Cleansing Department had come across a furry accident victim, a cat casualty on a city roadway.

Then, early on Monday afternoon, the Verger got in touch with news that an Anne Teak, from the Palace Street Gallery, wished to meet the Precentor. A free period at the school allowed Peter to go at once, and there he found a somewhat dejected, and decidedly dehydrated kitten – Mio graciously allowing himself to be reassured by his latest admirer. It seemed that, with business slack, the lady had taken a long weekend away, only re-opening her premises late that very morning. In so doing, she became half-aware of a strange, curiously husky sound, but one she could not trace. At the best of times, Anne was hard of hearing – even subject to *tinnutus* – and thought no more of the matter. However, when out to lunch at the Cathedral Tea Rooms, she read about the stray, and on return to the gallery did not take long to tune in to the croaking Siamese fugitive. Hoarse, but incredibly happy to be discovered in his dungeon cell, the kitten was duly returned and his Obliger obliged. Nor did the redoubtable Miss Teak claim the proffered reward, instead presenting the kitten with an expensive corded tassel as a trophy for fur endurance!

Mio's return to the Precincts was hardly a triumph, and although evidently delighted to have him home again, Peter did not rest until a collar had been placed round the kitten's neck. Anonymity was all very well for a resident, came the explanation for such discomfort, but paw-loose wanderers needed a clear statement of ID to safeguard Siamese status. Craddock himself had presented Peter with the collar, and, as if bound for a cat show, he took Mio next door to Anselm Hall where the Canon duly checked the band for size. They had been invited for tea; and at precisely five minutes past four, the reverend gentleman's housekeeper entered the drawing room with a tray full of treats for the multi-cat *ménage*.

Already well known to one another as neighbours, the cats exchanged greeting sniffs, chirruped away, and enjoyed the bounty Mrs Eves had bestowed. 'Miss Mong' – an attractive domestic shorthair, jet-black in colour, but with a white streak on her left flank – received a bowl of crunchies. Alight with delight, her little round face stared up at the Canon anticipating his customary slap with the softest mew.

"What a loose woman, showing your slip like that," Craddock confided as he patted her rear. In reply, Miss Mong purred away and yet, as was her custom, deferred until Ginger went to sample his minced rabbit. A patriarchal puss, Ginger commanded respect from all at the Hall; but slowed down by deafness and poor eyesight, the feisty old fellow took time to reach his dish. As for 'Sheba', elegant

Siamese Queen and the Canon's most treasured possession, she found Mio of greater interest than any saucer of
cream. For here in the royal presence was another Oriental,
an intact male who reminded her of past times and litters
long ago. For his part too, Mio found himself possessed by
the strangest of feelings, a surge that sadly subsided when
Peter chose to keep Sheba at bay as she sidled up to his
kitten. "Enough excitement for one day," was his comment,
and a sentiment the Canon seconded with a smile.

Mystified, Mio had to yield to his Obliger's firm
embrace, but petted and rubbed he soon relaxed enough
to purr, his reward a cheese square. Then, leaving Sheba,
Ginger and Miss Mong to their tea, Peter carried the
kitten into a library where the men had an entirely different agenda. Contentedly purring and at ease on his
Obliger's knee, the kitten could not have known that his
Canterbury days, already numbered, were fast slipping
away. Another move was planned, for Peter had been
offered a Cambridge post. And with amorous designs on
Sheba no longer a reality, Mio's second life slipped sadly
away. It was surely a kitty cadence, but one to which the
Canon gave a loud 'AMEN'.

3

*T*he discomfort of a collar was not the only pay-back resulting from that Canterbury tale and ill-fated rat roam. Indeed no – for I had to see Blount again! This time, with a snip-snip here and a snip-snip there, I was, as I'm told they say in the States, well and truly 'altered'. And even though my Obliger spoiled me rotten for several days, such a loss-of-life experience seemed a poor reward for my vigilant defence of 'the People'. Not long after too, the travelling basket reappeared to spirit me away to what was jokingly called a 'Catswold' retreat while the canine-human family moved to Cambridge. I will leave Peter to elaborate.

How generous of Mio to prompt his Obliger here, for without adequate explanation it might seem that Peter had chosen to neglect a six-month-old kitten – even to abandon the little fellow because of a mere career move. In actual fact that was far from being the case, every care being taken to ensure the best temporary home for a much-prized pet and avoid casual confinement to a cattery. If his Fellowship allowed Peter to live in College, Grace and the Corgis had to seek accommodation in the town until a suitable Cambridge home could be found for them all. Conveniently near Downing, Peterhouse agreed to the temporary lease of a flat in Fitzwilliam Street; and when the matter came before the Governing Body, the Fellows duly recorded that the two Corgis were 'deemed to be cats'.

Two Corgis note, for before they could leave Canterbury key tasks confronted the family. First of all, with much the same dilemma Jenny and her friend Anne faced in Danbury days, good homes had to be found for *six* puppies. Number seven, the only little girl, was not to be sacrificed. For BESS, albeit the runt of the litter, was clearly the kind of colourful character no family could spare, her close friendship with the kitten likewise endorsing the decision. Already known for their appearance in the *Kentish Gazette* too, her six brothers soon went their various ways; and this left Peter and Grace free to face their second task – a lodging for Mio.

Some years earlier, Grace had been seriously ill, surgery and physical weakness demanding rest and careful convalescence. At the time, a worried Peter took counsel from a colleague who recommended Grace to rural Gloucestershire where she went to stay with Mary Brazier in Coln St Aldwyns. Kindness itself, Mary was famed for her care, a consideration she extended to every creature that came her way. Although Grace naturally received priority from her hostess, she had never forgotten the way Mary cherished her pets, whether horses, dogs or cats. And with that memory in mind, it took only the simplest telephone call to arrange board and lodging for a Siamese evacuee. In short, well before the terrible upset of removal transported the household to Cambridge, Mio was driven to Gloucestershire.

There is a unique quality about the English countryside, and few fail to recognize the indefinable character that makes the Cotswolds its very heartland. By the standards of the British Isles, the area is large enough in scale; yet if much of it is internationally known, secluded spots still exist where even American visitors have yet to penetrate. The valley of the River Coln is one such shrine, for although the road that links the Oxfordshire town of Burford to Bibury is well enough known, the gentle trout stream that meanders from that Gloucestershire village to Coln St Aldwyns runs into comparative rural secrecy. And it was there, at Manor Farm House just off Main Street, that Mio, newly emerged from kittenhood, began his catalescence.

Taking over from Peter, Mary's warm welcome accepted the puss as no pariah, and his new life began. Emerging from the basket, the young cat needed to stretch after his travels, and did so with a bored yawn. Extending a hand by way of introduction, his hostess first received a some-what reluctant chirrup before, condescending to accept her caress, Mio deigned to rub against the good woman's knee. A gesture of delight for any experienced cat lover, it was also a hint informing Mary that here was a fur boarder sufficiently at ease to be offered the run of her spacious residence. And possessed of the freedom of the farmstead so to state, Mio soon began to savour scents from room to room. Inside he found food and comfort; and from a stair-head summit likewise surveyed an outside court encircled by stables and stores, with a stack yard beyond. He felt at home, and granted the high intelligence of his species, even experienced a whisker of *déjà vu* for Essex days. In the stack yard too, he met another lady – a fine grey cat whose orange eyes returned his gaze with surprising satisfaction.

No mere damsel in distress, Grey Cat went to great

lengths to size the little fellow up. After all, he was the first Siamese she'd met, and a lingering male odour prompted her to greet him with closed pads and open paws. Mio's youth was vastly appealing, however much, on closer examination, the lady realized that full courtship had no future. Instead, it was the kitten's inexperience that charmed her maternal instinct, and Grey Cat chose the role of foster-mother. What a break – for now at last the kitten could be trained in precisely the skills Turtle would have bestowed.

If their initial encounter took place in the farmyard, it was to her haunt in an old apple loft above the stables that Grey Cat led Mio for refuge. And in that intimate space the cats stared one another out. First, the kitten nosed Grey Cat. But pawed to the floor, he rolled over, and relaxed in submissive mood. When this prompted a well-nigh silent hiss, Mio began to play, dislodging a small apple and padding it into touch along the boards.

Although Grey Cat chirped approval, she preferred to sit and stare; and it was not long before the kitten's high spirits calmed down in response. Such silent appraisal continued in style as, comfortably crouched with paws tucked under, they took time to assess one another. Raised on a bench at one end of the loft, Grey Cat held court, while not far away, aping an exhibit of 'Still Life with Apples', the Siamese sphinx returned her gaze.

Precisely what the cats conveyed to one another, mere humans can only speculate. But authentic biography must at least provide the building blocks of life experience, and just as surely indicate their origin. From such a viewpoint

then, Grey Cat probably chose this moment not only to set
her new acquaintance at his ease – in itself no mean feat
when she faced a chatty oriental – but also to explain her
place at Manor Farm.

After losing kittens at one of those human 'Rescue
Centres', Mary had claimed her as a 'House Cat'. Soon
aware that this meant a life of pampered gluttony, mounting
frustration prompted Grey Cat to reclaim independence,
the very essence of feline character. Although in no sense
an ingrate, she was prone to flick her tail at constant fuss,
however much she found chin chucks fine, and readily
warmed to the occasional rub. Nevertheless a full round

of perennial petting, silly games and chatty palaver could only crowd out precious hunting time. Even humans regarded hunting as 'the sport of kings', so Grey Cat had no hesitation in reminding Mio that the chase simply had to be the birthright of any real cat. Accordingly when Mary produced an 'Activity Post' for her puss – a twee timber tower crowned with a catnip 'mouse' – Grey Cat was singularly unimpressed. She did her best to indicate that the very idea was patronizing to a skilled predator, and in determined mood began to bring back prey to show she could earn her own keep.

Exchanging further confidences, Grey Cat assured Mio that no cat could have done more to prove her worth. But when she had chosen to decorate the kitchen with a full range of dead birds, her efforts did not please. Perhaps Mary found feathers annoying and only chose ready-plucked fowl for the table? Nor did Grey Cat's hostess give thanks for the live mice she received – even those left for her especial use in the riding-boot cupboard. Clear that nothing tasted better than a succulent shrew, Grey Cat could not account for human displeasure at the reliable delivery service Mary had at her disposal.

But in a moment of high drama, it was her love of antiques that ended Grey Cat's career as an indoor cat. Regularly groomed on Mary's *chaise longue*, the puss purred and preened at leisure. In dire need of restoration, the period piece went off to be recovered. Immaculate on return – glowing with red velvet and well-nigh infused with an odour of sanctity – the sofa nevertheless lacked much of its former charm. To achieve this, Grey Cat carefully chose her moment, and while Mary rode out to Bibury, she did all in her claws to add finishing touches and complete the restoration process. A thorough spray could soon subdue the phoney fragrance of any furnishing fabric; and her talent with talons quickly softened rough surfaces to cushion the seat. Grey Cat did not deny that such professional attention left a trace of detritus, but steadfastly *affured* pools and shredded velvet piles as recognizable craft signatures throughout the cat world! And some 'love seat' it turned out to be too! For on Mary's return a baffling burst of human anger actually made that lady show her lover the door! Henceforth, although feeding bowls were generously replenished, they stood by the scullery to make Grey Cat an outsider.

With ears sharply focussed and attentive throughout, Mio felt humbled by the account. Grey Cat's welcoming cattitude made him feel at home, honoured that she had taken the trouble to afford an interloper sound advice. Never slow in the uptake too, he chose to follow her counsel. It was wise to recognize human foibles, and it could not be beyond feline wit to observe proprieties – the *fur*malities that would make her latest lodger Mary's ideal inside cat. However, to be confined to Manor Farm would condemn him as only half a cat; and to avoid Grey Cat's fate he must also explore. In short, as far as possible, Mio would divide his time. Indoor life promised every creature comfort: good food, warmth, and the sheer luxury of leisure to groom in peace. Beyond too, in the great outdoors, did not the call of the apple loft summon? For there in Grey Cat he had an ideal foster-mother, a senior cat ready and willing to hand down hunting skills. A single glance at those orange eyes revealed an impressive adult well able to instil the craft and cunning he sorely lacked. With but half a personality, he needed space. He needed her help as he strove for feline maturity, and knew she would not fail him.

It is, I must confess, a great comfort to learn that my Obliger was concerned enough to have at least some idea of what I faced when evacuated to Coln. At first, I naturally assumed he had abandoned me; but Mary's attention soon made clear that, far from being the case, Peter really had entrusted her to provide the best possible lodgings. Nevertheless, because feline care cannot be surpassed, it was of course Grey Cat's cautionary tail that alone made it easier for me to put my best paw forward as a Manor Farm insider. For repetition of the suffocating inside care Grey Cat had herself endured would kill any cat with kindness! So I chose to enjoy the best of both worlds. Mary simply had to be made aware that purrfection guaranteed model behaviour, and Siamese status gave me every right to come and go as I pleased. I certainly needed no human permission to depart for the apple loft and there sit at the paws of such a learned lady as Grey Cat! The cat's whiskers in terms of experience, she had much to teach me, as Peter can disclose.

How true – for an accurate account of Mio's life in the 'Catswolds', his deeds and misdeeds, would fill a book in itself. A summary must therefore suffice and allow full focus to rest not on life with Mary at Manor Farm, but on the great outdoor life the youngster experienced with Grey Cat.

If common parlance has offered the word 'twitcher' as undignified coinage for 'bird watcher', a proper parallel for 'catwatcher', duly dignified in the civilized language of the French, would be *chatellaine*! For Mary kept a close eye on her charge. And when added to observations from many a villager, her information provided a careful record of '*cat*ivity' in Coln. Routine apparently embraced both theory and practice, dividing the day accordingly. So once Mio had attended the apple loft for Grey Cat's course of basic instruction, he duly set off at dawn. Returning for breakfast, he would then sleep until it was time for a mid-afternoon appointment in the loft. And there the two cats stayed until sorties at dusk, Mio returning to the Manor well before Mary locked up for the night.

Grey Cat taught from instinct and experience and strove to impart true feline wariness. As she glared at her pupil in the apple loft, the golden glint of her eyes radiated independence and gave her instruction an authority that almost dispelled the gloom. Duly hypnotized, the kitten was first regaled with the playful side of hunting, the race of the chase, tail semaphore and the batting of butterflies and bees. But going way beyond anecdote, Grey Cat dealt with key skills and those field techniques essential to mature cat survival. For although most humans were happy to help – and if not they were easy to use – true cathood only came to genuine felines self-sufficient by right. However well cared for and fed, they had to make their own kill. Dogs might hunt in packs, and were stupid enough to hunt for humans. By contrast, the feline ideal was one of unique independence and cats hunted for none but themselves.

So much for theory: but what practice did Grey Cat recommend? With planning that amounted to paws-on preparation, she taught Mio to patrol a territory and build up an intimate knowledge of the gardens, fields and hedgerows bordering the farm. In expansive mood she showed him her own favourite haunts, and with rare generosity suggested they form a team. Hunting dogs were creatures of impulse, and the noise they made commonly checked conquest. All that barking Grey Cat dismissed with disdain. It was a hindrance to true hunting, a doggy deficiency that ran counter to the crucial element of surprise.

Tails of the unexpected gave full advantage to every cat, and Mio must learn the art of taking prey unawares. Just think of the spider, Grey Cat advised: familiar with her woven web, she hides away to emerge at speed once an insect is enmeshed. Similarly it is wisdom – the canny craft of cats – to act like sentinels carefully to spy out a situation, pounce, and take victims unawares. And Grey Cat cautioned the kitten of the need to keep quiet, rehearsing at length how he must keep silent and use stealth to ensure success. Claws should be sheathed until required – kept sharp and ever ready. Only unkempt dogs, impatient in the pace of the chase, were crazy enough to wear down their nails. Far better to survey the situation, and from a vantage point to lie in wait. If prey thinks it's safe to be out of sight, learn that it's *never* out of a good cat's mind! Remember the leap in the dark – that innate ability to jump five times our height from a standing start – not only adds the proverbial cubit to a cat's stature, but also reinforces the surprise of his pounce. And references to the art of climbing concluded the lesson to leave Mio inspired. Marvelling at Grey Cat's intelligence, and convinced that a combination of her guile and force must bring rich rewards, he resolved to achieve such prowess for himself. But it was time to take refreshment; return to Mary; and sleep awhile. So the cats arranged to meet again at dusk.

≋≋

Peter and Grace moved to Cambridge in September in good time for the start of the new academic year, so it was early Autumn when Mio first came to Coln St Aldyns to settle in with Mary. The annual upheaval of harvest had unsettled the natural world, and in fields where sheep did not graze, stubble strewn with grain yielded good returns for both birds and mammals. Albeit wary of Buzzards circling overhead, finches and sparrows used every opportunity daylight offered, just as Pheasants proudly filled their crops to glean a plentiful supply. If hedgerow cover also enabled the rabbit population to enjoy the sun, most mammals preferred to feast by moonlight when multitudes of mice and many another rodent set forth to forage above ground.

In terms of timing then, Greenwich was irrelevant and daylight saving a bore. Cat time came at dusk or dawn, to make afternoon siesta or pitch-dark slumber paramount as puss prepared to hunt. With sober vigilance a maxim, Grey Cat scorned a sleepy-headed Mio; and it was a young hopeful, obedient, wide-awake and ready for the fray who crept out to meet her in the half light.

A skilful predator, she soon caught a mouse, bowling it for her pupil to bat and learn how to kill. However lavish, Mary's diet was no excellent sufficiency for a young Siamese, and warm mouse blood the ideal supplement. Next it was his turn, and leading Mio to a tumbledown potting shed at the end of the garden, Grey Cat suggested he jump on raised staging for the best view of the floor. Cheered by his aperitif, and tantalized by swishing movements of his tutor's tail, kitten pawed cat in playful mood. Reproved at once with a deep-throated curse, he was told to concentrate. Such antics could only distract; vigilance was called for; and a combined attack demanded his full cooperation.

In no time at all too, a long-tailed Field Mouse scuttled into the shed. With forepaws outstretched Mio plunged on the quarry. A faint squeak betrayed doom as the fur missile struck, and prize in claw the champion celebrated his first success with a modest cry. Grey Cat's approval came fast to crown a lesson well learned: concentrate; secure; and play. For her, Mio's mouse died too soon. Recognized puss-cat precept dictated the catch, with squirming prey tightly clawed; playful temporary release, a time of practice to perfect the pounce; and then recapture, the moment to kill. In brief, seize, slapstick and slaughter. Humans never understand, but if there is another factor, it's surprise. First, the shock of the creature captured; secondly, that fascination at the reaction of prey temporarily released, the true cat-and-mouse game; and then the grand finale when life gives way to death. Just make the most of it, and always keep on your pads for instant action! Never mind that most humans tend to despise felines for precisely such foresight even though others have come to realize that, without their dutiful care, rodents would overrun the world. So do learn to be confident of ultimate cat supremacy, and remember that in Egypt long ago felines attained godlike status. Like mounting excitement in a kind of puss-cat polka, the reference brought Grey Cat's lecture to a climax; and with a flick of her tail she went back to the loft, leaving Mio time to return to Mary before lights out.

Back inside Manor Farm House, his hostess received an affectionate rub and the grateful mews expected from a lodger ready for supper. But after the meal Mio had more on his mind than the wonted wash-and-groom routine. In repose too, it was a snug little Siamese who replayed the day's excitement and looked forward to a future of versatile talent.

Eventful weeks followed to widen the hunting horizon, and guided by Grey Cat, Mio achieved much to perfect her practice. She warned him of the ferocity of cornered rats, and advised against going near Badgers. Foxes were different, but if a semi-feral cat like herself could insist on taking first helpings before any red rival, a cosset kitten with no real need to dine out should keep well clear of artful robbers. He had to be wary of Weasels; and was reminded that a Stoat family resided below bricks from a ruined summerhouse beyond the orchard. Both chased rabbits at high speed, but patience and well-placed poise above a burrow was preferable. For in their turn, cats enjoyed rabbit, and once skinned, their so-called 'kittens' made a welcome change from mouse, shrew or vole. By and large, Grey Cat found birds a bore; they rarely responded to play; and to be frustrated by feathers was sheer hell.

On the credit side, however, plucked pheasant or partridge was a different matter; and Grey Cat taught Mio that, in season, Catswold residents shot fine birds and left them to hang in cold, easily-accessible outhouses. With such bounty on offer, the cats lost no opportunity to help themselves. It had to be daylight robbery too, for even careless cooks checked doors at dusk. And if Grey Cat's camouflage had made such ventures undercover, the new Siamese thief stood out! Before long he was the talk of the village, particularly after Grey Cat had educated him in the art of tickling trout.

Yes *trout!* The fish were farmed locally, and always available for a tasty snack. Initially Otters – spotted by an angler, and absorbed in their favourite game of water polo – were held responsible for such plunder. But when a group of locals, chatting outside the New Inn, observed Mio, trout between teeth, sprinting down Main Street, blame fell squarely (and to humans fairly) on the cats! Even so, some saw fit to defend the felines on the grounds that their own pampered pets could not possibly cope with needle-sharp bones. For her part, however, Grey Cat was not to be patronised or compared with fastidious fur freaks. Proficient as a paw angler in her own right, she had not only taught Mio to fish, but also to fillet, and enjoy their 'catch of the day'! It was humans who made headlines by choking on fish bones, cats never. Caution ensured that no fish dish punctured puss-cat gut; and once humans learned to concentrate, to stop the chatter that seriously marred their every mealtime, they too could find the time to relish food, and to do so in safety.

Whatever their defence, however, the cats were not consulted, and the next round went to the village. It was no
surprise to find that, as a whole, the community frowned
on cat burglars; and once local worthies – the Women's
Institute in committee, and regulars who propped up the
Inn's public bar – began to compare notes, even cursory
stocktaking revealed a rise in petty theft. Briefly, Coln was
convinced that cat crime had risen, was rising, and had to
be diminished. Numerous solutions were suggested, and

whatever its primary purpose, no meeting of locals failed to register fury at a crisis of cats.

At the *Summer Fête*, for example, the Fortune Teller convinced all of imminent *cat*astrophe. An ancient fable foretold that the Devil himself implanted three hairs at the tip of every cat's tail, hairs that prompted pussies to prowl and yowl! And whether cutting cards, reading tea leaves or discerning those profitable coin-crossed palms, the Crone from River Cottage predicted chaos if Coln failed to tame its strays. Nor did she fail to give the fable a Siamese slant – an emphasis that exposed poor Mary's black-tailed lodger. To be accepted, foreigners must prove their worth; so why not frown on Mio, a displaced puss and yowler well known to prowl and pilfer?

Despite common knowledge that, unlike dogs, at law cats are classed as wild animals, some folk began to contemplate action. And convinced that the matter merited Parish Council attention, pressure groups prepared their case for the next agenda.

Coincidentally – far away in Cambridge, after almost a year of separation – Peter was ready to reclaim his charge. When he telephoned, Mary's relief almost rang down the wire, and an early date was agreed for the cat's collection. Warned in advance by the reappearance of his travelling basket, Mio took leave of his friend. Wishing him well, Grey Cat advised that he value the summons at this stage of a promising career. He should give no heed to superstitious nonsense; be mindful of her guidance; and make the most of any cat culture a college could offer.

My whiskers were retracted when I was reunited with my Obliger. The year had not aged him, but many months apart made me unsure of myself and uncertain of him. But as Peter held out a hand to sniff, I immediately sensed warm affection, and knew I had been missed. At Coln, human frailty almost wrought havoc on my plans. But Peter was sure to know the truth, and found no cataclysm in those Catswold days.

4

For a human hostess, Mary had certainly proved herself as a truly cat-conscious carer. As I left Coln for Cambridge, she could not even bring herself to pet me, but gave a longing look almost as if bereaved. Admittedly there was her horse; but although she rode regularly, and was privileged to enjoy occasional glimpses of Grey Cat feeding outside the scullery door, I knew she would miss the regular attention I had given as an insider of distinction. But just before he drove me away from Manor Farm House, I picked up a snippet of Peter's conversation to learn that Grace had already left, and was, as he put it, '…on the way with the wow-wows.' What could he mean?

By puss-cat standards, Mio was by now a seasoned traveller, and *en route* for Cambridge provided good company. Never lost for words, with many a mew to the driver, he gave a full running commentary on the journey. If he also made ready to renew friendship with Jane and Bess, he was to be disappointed. The Fitzwilliam Street lease had run out, and until the family's country home was ready for occupation, another Cambridge property served to house the family. A Pembroke hostel in Botolph Lane, this proved perfect for the puss, but all too crowded for Corgis as well. In short, to Mary's delight, Grace was to take the dogs to Coln, an ideal exchange for both parties at a difficult time.

Since the move from Canterbury, Grace had served Pembroke well as Nursing Sister, particularly when influenza struck. No respecter of persons, the epidemic afflicted both the Master and a certain Peter Cook. An M.A. of the University, Mio's Obliger was qualified to be a hostel keeper, and in line with the old regulations, able to guarantee residence qualifications for four men under his roof. The College owned various hostels for men living out, and Nos 2 & 3 Botolph Lane were particularly prized for their central location and proximity to Pembroke. If careful conservation preserved the early Victorian frontage, ingenious architect design from a Mr Harold Parker transformed the cottage interiors to provide ample accommodation. With the hostel keepers at No 3, three floors housed undergraduates at No 2, doors and corridors linking and uniting the properties as a single unit. Bounding a well-known bakery at the back, a bleak yard and roofscape was no place for a puss. But across the narrow lane to the front, the walled-cemetery garden of a down-town parish church was there to welcome any careful cat.

Mio settled down well, and once mindful of his Obliger's attention, lost no opportunity to get acquainted with the undergraduates. When Peter set off to teach in Downing, and Grace left passage doors ajar, he rarely missed the chance to steal into No 2 for a fur flirt with the men. Flattery got him everywhere, a Siamese yowl, quickly followed by a rub, a wink and what most residents took for a grin, soon secured admittance to bed-sitting rooms and the company he craved while his Obliger was away. Hugh Dakin thus found Mio a better companion than many a lion he had met in his native South Africa; and Mr Jeremy Firth could be relied on for a cuddle and cream. Only the

curious Mr Cusden, remote in his garret, seemed actively to dislike cats.

Then too, it did not take long to savour smells from adjoining premises, for next-door-but-one, at the lower end of the street, George Alsop ran a butchery business. Known throughout the City for their love of domestic animals, the Alsops added pet packs for regular customers; and with weekend joints came small parcels of neatly-chopped liver and lites to feed dogs and cats all over Cambridge. So an open door that gave access to the Lane gave an inquisitive Mio two main options; and depending on the time of day or night, it became his custom to visit either the butcher or the churchyard.

Acting as cashier to the business, Hilda Alsop sat in something of a sentry box. Positioned at right angles to the main counter, she faced the shop entrance and rarely failed to notice four-footed customers who came her way. A regular of course, Mio was happy to be smuggled inside, and there purred on her knee until reclaimed. In days when full food-shop fuss about hygiene was yet to come, what better solution for a temporary stray than tasty-meat morsels and knee-cushioned purrs? Well worth the effort, the one drawback to such visits was the telephone. Yet while bells rang for Grace to collect her fur deserter, there was usually time enough for a rapid cat snack.

Churchyard visits were different because, in early days at least, they were accompanied. Every morning, Mio was carried by his Obliger to the wicket gate and there admitted. As he tickled the cat and set him down, Mio was reminded that, as the only royal resident in Botolph Lane, he was privileged to enjoy full 'freedom of the Churchyard'. The perk made him purr before, frisking around at speed with tail at curve and swerve, the young cat sought to relieve himself. In the meantime, Peter's interest in ornithology allowed privacy; and reclined on a favourite table tomb, full fur ablutions were performed before breakfast. Only the clamour of bedmakers making for Queens' from the 'Bus station disturbed the peace; and perhaps prying eyes from an attic set, the fascination of Cusden ailurophobe?

At dusk, the routine was much the same except for a unique occasion when it was Mio's turn to meet the media. Challenged in the gloom, Peter was asked to explain himself.

"I'm here to collect my pet," he replied, "a cat currently fouling consecrated ground!"

A tale of the unexpected, the incident received prominence in the *Cambridge Evening News* when, on retirement, Mrs Morrison recounted highlights of her time as St Botolph's Lady Verger. Needless to state, Mio escaped to his beloved green space on numerous other occasions. It was simple enough to lie in wait and, lurking behind the front door, make a mad dash for the churchyard. As often as not he then distracted cyclists and tourists alike by use of the wall for fashion display, a cat walk in fact. When in the mood too, there was also time for serious church mouse-work among the tombs and monuments beyond.

The aged Rector, the Reverend C T Wood, B.D., Senior Fellow of Queens', held Mio in high regard as a St Botolph's celebrity. It was he who encouraged Warden Alsop to read Lessons; and when Peter trained George in Church, a Siamese presence dignified the audition. Positioned near the West door, a faldstool by the font gave Mio prominence and full view of the lectern. Hard of hearing himself, the Rector turned to the cat, and his juror did not fail the priest. With pointed ears alert, the sensitive Siamese evidently appreciated another eccentricity from his friendly butcher. Intelligence shone from the depths of his deep blue eyes, a lively sense of favours to come convincing the cleric that the candidate should pass his test.

Away from the Parish Church, Mio assumed other responsibilities inside the cottage. Pembroke College provided agreeable quarters for its hostel keeper at No 3 Botolph Lane. Neither spacious nor cramped, the rooms were essentially comfortable and afforded ample testimony to the architectural expertise that had transformed a space once merely two-up, two-down. Grace was pleased with her kitchen; and Peter had a little upstairs den – an invaluable extension to his main study in College – off the master bedroom. Decidedly his own fur self, Mio's wanderlust directed him from place to place according to whim. Trial and terror ordered many a day – his trial and Grace's terror!

However snug, any place by the fireside was no site for a Siamese. Mio preferred to position himself as a bookend, and adorned an alcove to the right of the stove. There he kept vigil in an ideal lookout post, and through the front window had full view of Botolph Lane. Contemplation of passers-by was crucial, and albeit at risk, Grace's ornaments and precious pieces of porcelain had low priority.

Although human pride later claimed the credit, CCTV was surely invented by cats and no lady of any house should question their role!

Dismayed, but by no means deterred by such Siamese insistence, Grace then purchased a fine cat bed for the prince. Draught free on raised legs, it was a grand affair designed by humans as a feline four-poster. Anything new was sure to secure Mio's attention, but approval was quite another matter. And with disdainful sniffs and a flick of his tail, the cat chose to occupy a grocery box instead, later disrupting routine housekeeping still further by bedding down in the washer drum!

Well trained in medical matters, Grace was loath to grant Mio bedroom access; and although he hugely enjoyed himself on his Obliger's knee to impede Peter's progress at the typewriter, the cat remained below at bedtime. Denounced by a rising crescendo of cat calls – pitiful mews leading to many a pleading yowl – this arrangement was not to last. Unsatisfactory from the start, it was not long before Mio turned it to his advantage.

❧

It had been a bad day for Grace. In addition to a number of medical crises in College, domestic affairs frustrated her system at home. Mr Cusden complained of 'cat ambush', and threatened trouble with a report to the Dean. And something was also wrong in the kitchen. So before he went off to lecture, Grace drew Peter's attention to a faint, yet distinct, smell pervading the room. That Mio was also aware of unusual aromas was clear from the cat's curious pose during breakfast. Perched on his high-legged stool, he normally used the time to restore sartorial elegance with patient grooming after his own morning meal. But on this occasion such Siamese stage show was replaced by anxious suspense. Tantalized and ill at ease, his whiskers twitched as, with ears alert, he sniffed the air. Petted by his Obliger and temporarily reassured, a measure of uncertainty nevertheless remained. This prompted him to stand tall to catch scents the family might not detect. He faced the sink, and strong disinfectant poured down the drain soon overpowered the stench. However, as events were to prove, it was a problem subdued, not solved, and much excitement lay ahead.

When night fell, and the weary human family retired, Mio left the sitting room for kitchen patrol duty. At first, silence was the order of the night: all appeared normal. But had not that smell returned? In darkness too, the hub of the house was eerily quiet with only a solitary flame from a gas water-heater to flicker on surfaces by the sink. Convinced that cats can see in the dark, humans exaggerate – though a glimmer of moonlight is enough. And albeit through glass, the new moon's faint beam gave a Siamese taught by Grey Cat to spurn superstition, the bearings he needed for action. Nor had he long to wait, for from the cupboard beneath the sink, and again from under the back door, the kitchen began to heave with scuttling creatures emerging to scour the floor in search of anything available. Mio had hoped for mice, and was sorely disappointed when 'roaches' came his way. He mused from his stool as they hurried and scurried below. Cockroach conferences gathered in dark corners to show their dislike of the light.

But what right had they to inspect a cat's feeding bowl? A leap to the draining board helped to survey a desperate situation. It was a vanguard that circled the floor, followed by a whole army of roaches outside the back door. Observed through the window, they crossed the yard from the bakery, and something had to be done. Because sheer weight of numbers ruled out playful pawing, command and control decreed direct descent the best form of attack. A leap in the dark followed not only repelling roaches, but also knocking down the stool; and the loud echoing crash proved a knell that summoned Peter to an insect hell! For in the kitchen, his Obliger found a Siamese as hard at work as any Lord High Executioner, biting and clawing horny cockroach heads for dear life.

Once electricity shone on the scene, most invaders fled. Bright fluorescent light was particularly hateful to their kind: it also revealed a corpse-strewn battlefield. Further casualties were to follow when Peter's slippers swatted the rearguard in retreat – a repulsive process that cracked horny creatures full of blood and guts. Offended by such sights, sounds and the offensive smell involved, Obliger and obliged cleaned up without delay. Pioneer-Corps Peter mopped the kitchen floor, and Mio commandeered a table-top HQ behind the lines. He sought puss-cat purity as never before. Rough tongues clean well and relieve tension in a cat, and as the cockroach crisis receded, Mio knew from instinct his need of such relief. He continued to groom the morning after the night before, another busy day when Grace called pest control, and Peter visited the bakery. In a sense, the outcome was predictable: the Council's cleansing officer puffed white powder into every crevice in the cottage; and grateful for Siamese surveillance, the ladies from *Fitzbillies* showed suitable gratitude to the cat. But it was of course in the sequel that Mio truly scored: Grace changed her mind and gave permission to him to sleep in the bedroom.

And about time too, for humans ought to know that feline sensitivity can source any scent! I must admit that I had not come across roaches before, but knew full well Grey Cat would not approve of their kind. As a Siamese sleuth, my suspicions were first aroused on a visit to Mr Firth's room. Friendly and hospitable to all who came his way (and especially to me whenever I called), Jeremy toasted tea cakes on a fork before the fire. Crumbs fell in the hearth and soon attracted cockroaches. So my first encounter came one winter evening when, purring and sleeping on his knee after another saucer-full of cream, I spotted an unknown scavenger chomping away. Before I could investigate, a fellow undergraduate dropped by for a chat and switched on the light. He teased Mr Firth for falling asleep at his studies, light and merriment making the creature scoot away. On another occasion, curled up in the warm – hurrah for an open airing-cupboard door! – I just managed to glimpse a flat brown body squeezing spiny rear legs into cracked plasterwork. In short, I was aware of a problem – 'a filthy favour' – some time before Grace complained about smells, and would make good use of my reward to services rendered. Truth to tell, the very thought of unlimited bedroom access was enough to make me purr.

❦

Mio needed no second invitation, and after the cockroach crisis began to spend more time upstairs than down. Since his arrival in Cambridge, he had in any case been much at home in Peter's little study. He believed in *rights* and did not recognize 'privilege'. Assured of every attention at his Obliger's typing machine too, he not only pawed proofs but added his monogram to many a message for Peter to post. So why not master what humans called the 'Master Bedroom'? There he took a particular liking to Grace's dressing table, and made up to the mirror. What a fine fellow he beheld there! Was he really so elegant, or was that a rival hidden behind the glass? When a probing paw uncovered the truth, a mix of relief and congratulation came fast. With a chirrup of self-esteem, he began to purr and then wash. And when the image washed as well, vanity became mutual admiration and the cat's morale was boosted by the wonder of it all.

These were also frantic days for Peter. Young dons had to publish or perish; and deadlines were there to be kept. With little secretarial aid, preparation took time; and before computers came to ease the process, much time was needed to stage a text's transition from early handwritten drafts to the final typescript any reputable house found acceptable. Invariably too, heavy teaching commitments and a full round of college responsibility crowded in to produce a situation similar to that experienced when journalists and editors 'put a newspaper to bed'. Indeed, limited space at No 3 Botolph Lane even had to make good use of the double bed! With the quilt in place, a sizeable surface was freed for chapters and copies to pile up side by side. And midnight oil was well and truly burned to prepare a piece of Tudor history for the press. It proved an ideal arrangement too, until Mio chose to exercise his role as Editor.

The cat was fast asleep when work began, carefully cushioned in his favourite tub chair. But in a trice, subtle slits in oriental eyes followed every manoeuvre. And once full vision judged Peter and Grace to be in dire need, with a yawn, a stretch and a leap, the Siamese emergency service landed. Carefully placed paper piles began to merge, and claws thoroughly kneaded the cover below. In turn, candlewick fabric clung to the cat and made a spectacular of Mio's intervention. For when he took another leap to free himself, the demonstration pulled both cover and contents to the floor. Once again chaos reigned, and lessons had to be learnt. So while Peter attempted to restore order, Grace carried Mio away to the study. Bedtime finally came when the task was complete. And in what was left of the night, *three* folk shared the bed, two of them exhausted, one elated. Having made his point, Mio purred it home with claws caressing the candlewick, and whiskers tickling his Obliger's face.

❧❧

Cambridge often experienced Indian Summers, and in balmy late-October days, Mio enjoyed nothing more than study. With University Full Term well underway, dons and undergraduates busied themselves in laboratories or libraries; and he in turn surveyed St Botolph's churchyard, itself a study centre for any cat. Regular exercise was taken as before, usually with, but sometimes without, his Obliger; and if not actually on patrol in the little parkland cemetery, responsible bedroom access enabled Mio to view it from afar. Healthy household management prompted Grace to lower the upper window as a matter of routine; and in a heat wave better ventilation was achieved with the lower sash raised as well. But done in haste, a little extra height gave access to a brave new world.

I'm glad Peter took the point, for although the station on the sill was a splendid viewpoint, a cramped, narrow ledge did not compare with that box of flowers on the other side of the window! There, well supported by a wrought-iron basket, I could observe at leisure and catch the soaring scents from my own game reserve!

Ever aware of the risks involved, mere humans surely have to marvel at feline confidence. This was in no way shared by Grace, and a worried Nursing Sister had chance

to wish the cat a charmed life. Returning from a medical surgery, she first spotted Mio as she walked up King's Parade. A feature in itself, her window-box gave colour to Botolph Lane and contrasted well with the 'flamingo' paint Mr Parker had chosen to coat the wrought-iron basket. But now, with a discernible difference of tone (not to mention the moan she heard), the scene had changed. Crudely displaced, the morning's show of trailing geraniums had parted to reveal a new feature. For statuesque among the plants, a fur face shone forth, and as it stared, a chocolate countenance spluttered and swore whenever Sparrows and Starlings flew past.

Enlivened and eager to tell of his adventure, it took no time to coax the cat inside. If Blackbirds could eat their fill from the Church crab-apple tree, should he not complain? And if only their ears could catch the pitch, humans would surely condemn the screaming sound bats made at dusk!

After the window-box incident – and was it not appropriate for royals to make a balcony appearance? – Mio's movements were closely monitored, and it became more difficult to reach the churchyard without an Obliger in attendance. This had both advantages and disadvantages. It was certainly useful to be carried safely across the narrow lane. The crossing was hazardous as, when late for lectures, racing undergraduates on bicycles were the curse of Cambridge. But to have a human around when you hoped to hunt was an unwarranted handicap. Even so, the very sight of Blackbirds gorging autumn apples provoked a planning session: such fat fowls must roost at night and fur foresight suggested strategy for a prowl. When intel-

ligence and a house-to-house search made clear that geta-way from No 3 was barred, tactics suggested weakness on the hostel's student side. And just by the door of No 2 lurked trouble, waiting and ready to run! Cat-conceived, the plan was simplicity itself: a friendly face to attract; a mew and a rub to distract; a leap through the half-closed door and freedom!

It worked a treat; and once across Botolph Lane and over the boundary wall, Mio made for the apple tree and began to climb. Although empty of birds, branches provided stability and a goodly roost. The higher he went too, the better the view. Why restrict Cambridge 'Night Climbing' to the student world? He'd heard his human friends boast of roof-top skills – and even learnt of unknown heroes who, unseen, had once assembled a car on top of the Senate House. Now it was his turn, his challenge to scale a really high wall behind the tree. Clinging ivy was handy for claws; and in defiance of gravity, he dragged himself aloft, and with a series of upward leaps secured the summit. What an achievement! What fascination from flittermice too, as bats above and bats below wheeled and squealed around to pass on praise! Prowess indeed, for with such a panoramic view his puss-cat perspective paralleled Piranesi!

Per ardua ad astra to be sure – but it was not to last. Instead, with an explosive hiss, a disreputable alley cat entered the scene, a war-torn warrior determined to repel any rival who dared to trespass on his territory. Youthful and inexperienced, Mio barely stood his ground. He knew he was no match for such a pugilist; and already wounded with a ripped ear, he took no further risk. To descend the way he had arrived was out of the question, so he leapt to safety in a garden beyond the wall and there claimed sanctuary in a fine-limbed ornamental tree.

⁓⁓

It was almost time for Compline; and mindful of prayer on a calm night, Brother Barnabas began to make his way to St Bene't's Church. But as he left St Francis' House in the direction of Free School Lane, pandemonium banished any prospect of peace. In a daze, the otherworldly Friar first heard cries from souls condemned to purgatory; but when reality dawned on his senses, Barnabas witnessed mere terrestrial terror. For high above, on top of the twenty-foot wall across Botolph Lane lay the cause. A vicious fight progressed as felines, furred up to twice their normal size, caterwauled away to shatter silence and disturb the night. The Friar recognized the alley cat at once. True disciples of St Francis, he and his brethren had done their best to find veterinary care, to feed and tame the mangy creature. But was not the sparring partner Peter's young Siamese? It must be at risk, and there was just time to alert the Brooks if he made a detour down the Lane to reach St Bene't's by way of Trumpington Street.

Fully conscious of the crisis, Peter faced a real dilemma. From the Friar's account, he concluded that Mio had fallen from the wall. Nowhere to be seen in the churchyard too, his cat must be in the garden of Corpus Lodge beyond, and in trepidation he raced to Free School Lane to find the entrance. That this was an emergency he did not doubt. Yet to make an uninvited late-night call on the Master of a Cambridge College was a daunting prospect. Moreover, at the rear of the Lodge, the neo-Gothic doorway humbled him further with its offer of *two* bell pulls: *Visitors* or *Kitchen*. A dim light on the kitchen side eased his choice, and as a distant sound rang out, lights brightened and bolts were drawn. The door ajar, an elderly woman challenged in cultured tones:

"And what, may I ask, do *you* want at this time of night?"

Sotto voce and apologetic, came Peter's faltering reply: "…my cat!"

Acceptable and unquestioned, it was as if his two words had uttered *open sesame* and been a password! Admitted at once, he began to explain himself to Lady Thomson. A cat lover who clearly cared, she summoned her spouse without delay, and the Master emerged from his Study. Son of 'J.J.', and eminent in his own right as Professor of Physics, Sir George took charge. The full glare from chandeliers in the grand drawing room shed light on the garden; and there in a tree was a pitiful sight. Famed for his aristocratic accent, the Master's reaction was memorable: "I say, a cat in a crow's nest, wot!"

Accurate enough as an observation, his remark was strangely telling for two reasons. First, Sir George's *Who's Who* entry recorded a passion for 'Model Ships' under *Recreations*; so here was a man who knew a 'crow's nest' when he saw one! And secondly, how appropriate that Mio's choice of refuge turned out to be an Indian Bean-Tree – a *Cat*alpa!

Rescue effected, Lady Thomson warned Peter of what she chose to call 'cat leprosy'; and fearful of the threat a mangy mongrel posed for such a splendid Siamese, she felt Botolph Lane to be unsafe for Mio. So churchyard life had to end, for no responsible Obliger could allow his cat to court disaster.

5

*J*ust when I was making the most of my 'Freedom of the Churchyard', Peter decided to move me. He presumably had good reason – and as far as I recall was influenced in his decision by Hilda Alsop and a Tutor from Peterhouse. But for me it was another life lost. The little green space of that down-town cemetery had become a happy hunting range; and St Botolph's churchyard wall my parade ground. I had got to know both well; yet almost overnight I became a displaced puss-cat and was taken to Downing.

What a contrast! In place of intimacy – a small space where a young Siamese prince felt truly at home – immensity confronted me. Inside I shared the Dean's rooms in West Lodge; and outside my College life was bounded by Wilkins' great 'Quadrangle', a vast paddock, car parks, three impressive gardens, and what I chose to term a 'true wilderness'.

I could go on, but have already refused such a tedious task. So it must be time for my Obliger to continue his cat chronicle.

❦

Informed of feline 'mountaineering' and a late-night foray in the garden of Corpus Christi Lodge, Hilda Alsop came round at once to offer advice on the future of her favourite visitor. While George was left to cope with the butchery business, she attended to cat blood and examined Mio's ripped ear. A lady of no mean experience, Hilda knew her first aid and recommended saline solution as the best remedy. After some messy moments – for irritated, the cat's reaction was to shake his head so wildly that, liberally sprayed with gore, the cottage kitchen rapidly resembled a crime scene – the healing process began. But Hilda's worry did not end there. A true 'cat lady', she realized the risks involved in any future confrontation with 'that flea-ridden feral creature up the Lane'! Devoted to the work of her favourite welfare organization – the *Cats' Protection League* or *CPL* – she had not only raised considerable sums from 'Coffee Mornings' and sales like 'Bring and Buy', but also advised on the re-homing of many *protégés*. In the knowledge that the Brooks were soon to move into the County too, she proposed a spell of College life. Hilda knew a Fellow of Peterhouse who kept cats in College, so could not Downing both save the Siamese and the day? The very idea had instant appeal, and if implemented was sure to safeguard her fur friend.

～

An ornament to his Faculty, Mr E J Kenney was Director of Studies in Classics at Peterhouse. That he was also Tutor gave him fine rooms in College, a set that opened on to the Fellows' Garden. And there lived 'Fuff-Fuff', a tabby shorthair of uncertain birth, but a cat justly proud of her precious ringed tail. The oldest College in Cambridge, Peterhouse was a select society where Fuff-Fuff flourished, ever eager to contact any Petrean who came her way. When Secretaries looked for letters, a purring presence presided over the Office in-tray; and when Porters collected the post, the out-tray proffered an unobliging paw. And when, in

Easter Term or after Tripos, Tutorial parties were held in the Fellows' Garden, Fuff-Fuff made herself a star. Liquid refreshment undergraduates could keep to themselves; but they simply had to be taught how to share *canapés*. So with splendid tail aloft she sailed around and took over. All kinds of tasty morsels came her way, and in no time at all the Tutor's 'happy hour' turned into a furry interlude.

Good customers of the Alsops, the Kenneys often paused to report the latest news of Fuff-Fuff the feline celebrity. And when in turn Hilda told Peter, he lost no time deciding on a Downing refuge for Mio. His ground floor set in West Lodge faced Wilkins' great 'Quadrangle' full square. At the back too, because the window opened on to the garden, the bedroom could offer every convenience to a cat. So why not act at once? With the College barely a quarter of a mile distant, transport presented no problem; and secure in his basket Mio was carried away without delay.

Rare in itself, a free morning was not only a boon but entirely suitable to start the settling-in process. Fearful lest new surroundings subject Mio to further stress, Peter allowed the cat to leave the travelling basket in his own time. In no way weary from such a short journey, they blinked at one another. Owl-like on a swivel, the Siamese head surveyed the room. Its scale and Regency grandeur appealed, especially the view from two sash windows, elegant and tall with period glazing bars. Fine curtains hung down in folds to conceal him, and the cat could stare out at all who passed; and once reassured by a brief walk about, observation became his priority. If an Obliger chose to fill bowls for food and water, and position that litter tray,

new surroundings demanded that a cat practise security and attend to neighbourhood watch!

Ever the convivial cat, Mio was soon at home, ready to enjoy a sandwich lunch on his Obliger's knee. And that afternoon, relaxed in an armchair with post-prandial purrs, he attended his first Supervision. A knock at the door announced the pupil's arrival; and from his desk the Dean welcomed Mr Sylvester. Well dressed with folder in hand and clad in an undergraduate gown, the young man had prepared a piece on the Tudor revolution in government. Pleasantries exchanged, and motioned to a chair by the fire, a dutiful student began to read his essay. He'd found it a pressurized week, and aware of omissions, Sylvester expected interruption at any time. That, after all, was the Supervisor's role; and although new to the system, here was a freshman who valued one-to-one tutorial teaching in his development as a young historian. But when interference came, it was not the Dean who spoke: it was a chirrup from an alien source as a Siamese Supervisor took over to land on his lap. They had not been introduced, and intent on reading well to disguise the weakness of his prose, Sylvester had not seen the puss. For his part, however, Mio had spotted the student, and in him recognized a cat lover who, even if half-hidden behind a kind of paper shield, must welcome attention from another friend. Instead embarrassment all round brought the session to a sudden halt. Human laughter erupted and, temporarily at least, drowned loud purrs of approval.

"He certainly likes your essay!"

It was the Dean who spoke, and once clear that his pupil had no fear of cats, asked Sylvester to proceed.

The afternoon saw other pupils come and go, but Mio took little interest in their supervision. Rather did his attention turn to exploration, and in the window, he used the time to groom and gaze across the Court. When the last pupil left, to reward the cat's patience Peter took his pet to meet the Head Gardener. In the early evening, Hector Filkin returned to his greenhouse to take stock of the day. A senior College Servant, he checked the mowers and made sure his under-gardeners had cleaned and oiled the many implements in regular use. Before he left for home too, this was also Hector's quality time, his moment to check up on 'Susie', the College cat to whom he was devoted. An enchantress by character, Susie was a friend of the entire world. With her bright ginger coat, white mouth, chest and socks, she was singularly petite. Decidedly frail too – twenty years old with over three hundred kittens to her credit – she relied on Hector who always stayed to settle her down for the night in the heated greenhouse. His duty done, Mr Filkin had closed the door just as the Dean arrived.

"My word, Sir," he said with surprise, "where did you get that cat?"

With time to spare, the two men enjoyed a jaw; and while they did so the cats eyed one another through the glass. Impressed by Peter's lively account – how crowded a life for such a young cat – Hector told the Dean of Susie's latest conquest:

"You remember Dr Perry? He taught History here a'fore you came, and he has 'Candy'!"

The Dean knew Perry well enough, but at a loss to recall a former colleague's fondness for sweets, inquired further of Hector. The old man laughed, and as he stroked the Siamese explained that 'Candy' was Susie's kitten, the last of a long line, and…

"A lovely little critter the good doctor had taken up north to a University job in his home town."

Well pleased that Candy would be cherished, Hector went on to welcome Mio. He shared the Dean's view that such a fine cat was good for the domus, and knew Susie would make him feel at home. Territorial rights need not concern so aged a queen, and as a team the gardeners were always on guard.

I took to Hector at once. As a human he had respect and the right approach to a cat. First of all, he extended an index finger for me to sniff; and when I went ahead and nosed it, he knew he could chuck me under the chin. My Obliger always greeted me in precisely that way; and when I rolled over with delight, he tickled my tummy too and sent me into ecstasy! But no stranger could expect such a treat; and during my meeting with Downing's Head Gardener I was in any case held tight in Peter's arms. Even so, with a wriggle and a claw I climbed up on to his shoulder to get a better view of Susie behind glass. It gave Peter a fur stole and me a golden opportunity to learn the layout of the gardeners' base, replete with hot and cold glasshouses, frames, sheds, bins and a whole area reserved for mounds of compost, leaves, grit, peat and sand where you could recognize a rodent retreat without being the slightest bit nosey! No wonder Susie had agreed to make a GHQ of Hector's greenhouse!

A bell tolled: it was time to return Mio to West Lodge before Chapel. He had enjoyed his first guided tour and seemed content to settle in a fireside chair while the Dean went to Evensong. There were no callers, and returning before Hall, Peter found the cat in a deep sleep – at least until an affectionate pat prompted Mio to stretch and yawn. Accepted as a gesture, Peter had permission to leave for High Table and went off to join the Fellows at dinner. But after the meal, the Dean decided not to take dessert with colleagues in the Combination Room. In conscience he expected his cat to be lonely and, as if kitty himself had called, went back to his rooms.

Mio had not moved, and the precious hours gained, the Dean put to good use. In need of that finishing touch, next morning's lecture lay on his desk; there were essays to mark; and a book to review. Of no mean import too was the realization that his Bedmaker knew nothing of the cat. A telephone call to Grace explained the situation: once again Peter would spend the night in College. Responsible for discipline, he often did so, and many events kept him on duty. A round of dinners highlighted the social and sporting year; and a Downing success in 'Bumps' or 'Cuppers' always resulted in revelry. On such occasions, high spirits were one thing, but disruptive behaviour quite another; and any responsible College Officer had to be present, support the Porters, and keep the peace. However, it was a rare event for a Cambridge Don to pernoctate for a puss, and Grace's co-operation all the more appreciated.

That night men resident in College beheld a Siamese patrol. For as they left the JCR, the Library or the Bar, there on the lawn was the Dean closely followed by his cat. It was a cold night with a full moon, and as so often in Downing, a patchy blanket of low-level mist shrouded the great grass plot. No more than waist-high to a Fellow at walk on the grass, such murk largely covered the cat. Viewed from afar, what a pair they made. Most haled the Dean's familiar figure; but others found occasional glimpses of a black tail that hovered on high a curious sight. Not so Sylvester who came at once to greet his new friend; and the three of them went on to West Lodge garden where, after choosing to rub and purr round a sculptured stone griffin, Mio matriculated as a true Downing man. After the undergraduate declined the Dean's invitation for a night cap – Sylvester had another essay on the stocks! – all went to their rooms. When lights were extinguished too, curled up on the eiderdown a well-contented cat purred his Obliger to sleep.

～～

The Bedder showed up at 8 a.m. She rattled the oak and crashed the Dean's inner door. Opened correctly, the entrance was ample; but barely ajar it impeded progress and served to shatter silence as buckets and brooms banged against the wooden frame. And that was the point: arrival had to be announced. Once known for stealth, undergraduates had come to call her 'Ambush'. Of advancing years and unattached, she thrilled at the sight of naked young males, and likewise complained whenever a man "… 'ad a woman in 'is room." A reputation that required reform, it duly received the Housekeeper's reprimand. But unabashed, the Bedder's revenge was a noisy arrival calculated to wake the dead with a thunder roll.

Mio had heard nothing like it, and despite soothing sounds from his Obliger, thought it wise to take cover. He leapt to the floor and hid under the bed. And there he stayed until Peter had explained the presence of a cat in the set. No respecter of persons, 'Ambush' took umbrage at once:

"I've got enough to do without 'aving any pets about," she said, drawing heavily on a hand-rolled cigarette.

"And for my part," said the Dean, "I must repeat my request that you refrain from smoking in my room."

When the Bedder retreated into the kitchen, he got his reply:

"And I'm not 'ere to wash up your crocks! I've got *doctors* on my staircase, and it takes me all my time to see to them."

A reference to the Director of Studies in Medicine, the comment was intended to rile the Dean. But he had already withdrawn to the bathroom and, once dressed, retrieved the cat to take Mio for a morning walk in the Fellows' Garden.

When they returned, both doors remained open; and with a kitchen in disarray and the bed unmade, routine tasks were incomplete. Worse, when stale cigarette smell tainted the air, a flattened fag-end on the lavatory floor was evidence enough of a smoker's defiance. The Dean had been challenged, and needed to act without delay. But cats had priority, and, after due fuss, Mio was fed. Once the doors were secured, and the bedroom aired, he left for the

SCR. There he customarily perused the press, and made the most of a rare opportunity to keep himself informed before teaching took over, or the tyranny of the trivial demolished the day. This morning too, at an appropriate hour, he intended to call on the Housekeeper.

A College treasure in every way, Mrs Sandham had served Downing to the best of her ability for more years than she cared to recall. Bedmakers came, and Bedmakers fled; but she went on for ever. Experienced and shrewd, she not only knew her team but was also aware of the problems they faced in keeping undergraduate rooms clean. Dons could also be difficult, and when the Dean arrived she wondered what was up. Had he come to report more moans from the men? Was he about to relay the latest JCR protest? Or was it time for a pastoral visit, for kind words to help perseverance in tedious tasks? A stern demeanour suggested displeasure, and his purpose was stated with barely a pause:

"Good morning, Housekeeper. I won't waste your time, and come with a basic request. I simply wish to exchange my Bedmaker for a Hoover!"

"Really," Mrs Sandham replied. Arrested and astounded, she was oft to recall the occasion as a unique moment in her life of service to the College.

≈≈

On return to his rooms, the Dean met a College Porter who had just delivered the mail. Settled at his desk and distracted by numerous letters and a long-awaited journal,

Mio's absence failed to register. But once it did, a measure of panic set in. The cat seemed to have vanished: his favourite chair was empty; he had not concealed himself behind the curtains; and in the kitchen even his feeding basins were missing. If the bedroom also lacked any Siamese presence, a half-made divan and a wide-open window testified to what had been a very different presence. Outside too, clearly visible on West Lodge lawn, lay food and water bowls; and covered by a mat, what looked from a distance like an upturned litter tray. But there was no cat in sight.

Without a back door, access to the garden via the West Range of Wilkins' great 'Quad' took time; and by hastening on his way, it was a breathless Obliger who arrived on the scene. Shrubs surrounded the lawn, and a thorough search demanded scrutiny of a high order. Bright morning sunshine – filtered through leafy shadows in the borders – eased exploration, however much the closest inspection failed to reveal the Dean's missing treasure. Birdsong apart, the garden was silent. A gentle breeze rustled branches, yet Mio had found no hiding place in what was once the outer sanctum of F W Maitland and the 'Laws of England'.

To the south, a path led to the service yard where the Dean found a well-known Kitchen Porter. Ever ready to rest awhile, a halt was called to the on-going clatter of bins, and the figure of Eddie Froggett emerged for a chat. Something of a simpleton but nobody's fool, Eddie was normally the merriest of men. He fed the birds with stale toast to greet their greedy rivalry with many a laugh. Yet it was more in misery than mirth that he greeted the Dean:

"'e got a bird, Sir… 'e got a bird! One of me pigeons it were… one of me pigeons!"

If he felt for the man, Peter was more interested in Froggett's sighting than the fate of any pigeon. The culprit could well have been Mio; and with no time to lose, if only he could calm the situation, he might learn more. But Froggett remained in a high state of shock, and was not to be consoled: he grieved for the bird, and hated the cat:

"'Twas a young 'un, that pigeon, a dove of peace, not war! It 'adn't a chance; crept up on from be'ind a bin it were," Froggett continued. "Not fair to a young 'un. And when I banged with me broom, 'e didn't give up, 'eld on to me pet, and fled off raund theyre."

Grateful for the clue, the Dean tried comfort and a quick getaway. But Froggett had the hump, and his wry face a mixture of grief and sheer fury, he shouted:

"Make sure you get the bugger… Sir!"

Peter had clearly been given his marching orders, orders that echoed after the Dean as he crossed the service yard to round the SCR and head for the Fellows' Garden. Bounded by Tennis Court Road to the right, it was hedged off from the College Paddock to the left, and provided a large park and woodland acreage of rural calm. For such a central Cambridge location, it had a fine selection of specimen trees, a mini-arboretum renowned for cedars of Lebanon. And in such scenic splendour the Dean began to search for his cat. Good fortune helped to make the task straightforward: plumage that had once borne the wretched bird aloft now left a visible trail on the ground. Here and there feathers on the grass plot, a dotted line of grey on the green lawn that encircled weeping branches of the famous copper beech. Beneath the tree, against the bole, lay an expired Collared Dove. The victim of an absent assailant, the dead squab was hardly touched. Not far away, however, from a cedar tree, a spotless leopard called. Unending in sequence, proud impenitent yowls not only laid claim to the kill: they also betrayed the phantom presence that was Mio! With a sense of sanctuary too, he was a cat well placed; and just below his perch stood a sign – PRIVATE: FELLOWS' GARDEN.

〰〰

The reader should note that my outcry was intended to greet my Obliger. Noisy pests, pigeons are easy prey and cats take no pride in their kill. If Eddie really wanted a pet, he should aim high and choose a cat!

Considering what I'd gone through too, it was a cry of relief. For as soon as Peter left our room, the Bedder returned in a foul mood. Bored by her chores, she needed some fun, and I jumped on her brush to ambush 'Ambush' for a joke! It didn't work, and instead of a game, she threw the dustpan at me. It was time to withdraw, and when spray from a can followed me to the bedroom, I managed to squeeze out under the window.

Then came her shy: bowls were flung at me out of the window. That wasn't a game at all, but plain cruelty to cats. Such things are meant to try us, and they do! So while the Bedder fumed, I went on my way and took revenge on a brainless bird that happened to be in the right place at the wrong time!

〰〰

Life at Downing was not all high drama for the cat, and in the week that followed Mio settled into a sound routine. Well fed and watered, he claimed the slightly raised lower sash of his Obliger's bedroom window to come and go as he pleased. Readily recognizable as a College character too, wags deemed him worthy of mention in the University *Resident Members' List*. If he missed the freedom of St Botolph's Churchyard, that had been exchanged for patrolling rights in the Fellows' Garden, as good a deal as a cat could have. Unimpeded in fact, he had full scope to explore and hunt at will; and with time on his paws, so to state, made many an opportunity to get acquainted with Hector's Susie. He respected her age and experience, just as she admired his youth and encouraged any spirit of adventure.

⤳⤳

As Director of Studies, the Dean did his best to entertain all Downing historians socially, and after Supervision it was often his custom to ask pupils who came at *three* to stay for tea. Shortly after meeting the cat, Sylvester's turn came round. A bright man, he had written a particularly good piece, an *alpha* essay that marked him out as a rising Tudor scholar. Cheered by congratulation and rewarded with refreshment – *Fitzbillies* Chelsea buns ('probably the stickiest in the world'!) washed down with Darjeeling – conversation ranged widely. Feedback from University Lectures, new accessions in the Seeley, and other concerns of Clio, Muse of History, naturally had priority; but foreign travel, the Cambridge *Footlights*, and music also received *en passant* attention. Then, all of a sudden, and as if on cue, the mention of *music* was amplified with 'noises off'! Unique offering in repetitive form, a Siamese sonata mewed through from the bedroom to demand immediate investigation. Loud scratching raised the volume to fever pitch, and scurrying along the passage linoleum Mio dragged a Slow Worm into view. Long since dead, the unfortunate lizard – found buried in Susie's compost heap – had been brought home in triumph and to please, its arrival well and truly timed.

What followed proved altogether memorable. As he stroked the cat, and admired the trophy, the Dean inquired:

"Mio, what have you done?"

Confused, Sylvester replied:

"I don't understand, Sir?"

At first, with no wish to become the butt of a donnish dig, the young man suffered; but when it dawned that this was a meeting of *Mios*, he was highly amused. At that time, only Dons at King's called men by their first name, and Sylvester could not understand why the Dean should suddenly address him with a given name the young man hated. Best friends used his second name; and without wishing to cause offence, he failed to understand why so splendid a Siamese should also suffer 'degradation'! The Dean briefly explained the situation. He and his wife had continued to use a nickname the cat knew as a kitten, but in due time fully intended to give the matter careful thought.

By now, assured of praise and almost ready to be gazetted in an honours' list, the Siamese subject had left the lizard and begun to wash and groom on Sylvester's knee. He realized he was under discussion, and had never tolerated decisions *in absentia.* Long convinced that naming a cat was no commonplace skill, the Dean was delighted with recourse to a second opinion, and glad to enlist the prowess of a lively and sympathetic pupil. Not long since, he had praised Sylvester's work: an exercise commendable not only for content and analysis, but also distinguished for presentation and good style. And it was almost in supervision mode again that Sylvester was questioned:

"Would you agree that naming is ultimately a test of literary power?"

As he continued to pet the cat the student agreed. And barely audible above interference from continuous purring, the Dean recalled the Samuel Butler test:

"Think, Sylvester, of that man. Superbly lettered himself, he held it to be far more difficult to name a kitten than to write an inscription. Indeed, if I am correct, he wrote that by such a test, he was himself condemned, for he could not!"

It was the undergraduate's turn to contribute:

"I see the point," Sylvester said, "and when a Sixth-Former keen on brass-rubbing as a hobby, I often marvelled at good *grave* humour and its economy of style!"

The erratic snarly purr that followed – albeit the result of turbulent air flow – indicated a good joke enjoyed by all. It also pinpointed a puss who needed a name to which his career had already given meaning in no small measure. Sylvester again:

"You mentioned, Sir, your cat's interest in the chase, in rodents and even trout. And now with a College pigeon, and this Slow Worm to his credit, a hunter's name is surely appropriate?"

Impressed, the Dean agreed, and Sylvester went on:

"You remember the Old Testament lesson I read in Chapel at Evensong last Sunday?"

"I do indeed. Scholars rarely survive Hebrew genealogy without a slip! Fellows present were impressed by your clarity of diction, not to mention the assurance with which you persevered to pronounce your way through 'the generations of the sons of Noah'! And your friends must have hoped to tease a man who failed to get his tongue round such ghastly names as 'Ashkenaz, Riphath and Togarmah', not to mention 'Sabtah, Raamah and Sabtechah'!"

The Dean paused – he mused to himself that few Chaplains could stay such a course – but then demanded Sylvester come to the point. With a question, his reply came at once:

"Could I borrow a Bible, Sir?"

A wide gesture followed:

"By all means – there's an *A.V.* on my desk."

And with the cat clutched tight, and the place duly found, Sylvester began to read:

"'And Cush begat **NIMROD**: he began to be a mighty one in the earth.

He was a mighty hunter before the LORD.'

No pedigree puss, you tell me Dean; but these verses – 8 & 9 – from *Genesis* Chapter 10, can surely relate to your cat, and supply the sort of status symbol he needs?"

"Bravo, Sylvester, I think you've got it! I certainly consent and feel sure my wife will agree. Let's endorse your splendid idea with a well-earned glass of Sherry!"

It was an eager retort; and fully satisfied, a certain Siamese purred in unison as he crunched a nibble.

I found it a great pleasure to be treated with such deference! Fully recognized at last, the very sound of my new name gave me a sense of puss-cat pride! Never more content than when hunting too, I felt Sylvester's suggestion would have secured Grey Cat's approval just as it clearly delighted my Obliger. The Squire of Danbury's 'Mio' was decidedly unpleasant and a definite misnomer. We Siamese have real vocal talent, and steadfastly disdain caricature. It will take a little time to get used to 'NIMROD'; but a lifetime should suffice.

≈≈

For the Fellows, the election and arrival of a new Master is, by any standards, something of an occasion in the history of a College. Rivalry between external and internal candidates for the Headship of a House can be bitter; and although any successful candidate must secure the majority vote laid down by statute, significant dissent often remains to constitute minority opposition to the new regime. First impressions make or mar such occasions; and in a rare moment of inspiration, Downing's new Master decided, quite literally, to *descend* on the College! If other Cambridge Masters came on foot, or alighted from a river barge, he would come by air and use the furthest area of Wilkins' uncompleted 'Quad' as a 'helipad'. It caused a stir, and certainly made the kind of College spectacular most approved. The very personification of compromise, the new man duly moved into the Lodge and took up residence *with a dog*! By tradition this was not allowed, even to one who, as he often phrased it himself, "lived over the shop." However, as if by grace and favour, the Fellows deemed canine, feline; and most mornings after nine, the Master and his lady walked their pet pooch round the Court.

Senior cat by far, Susie had her views, and from experience knew a good cat when she saw one. In turn too, Nimrod made clear his disapproval of a wire-haired Dachshund on parade. How could humans – supposedly mature humans of high intellect – possibly deem such a low-strung creature to be *a cat!* And by standards newly set by 'Tiger' – a frightening feline who, about this time, had chosen to claim the College as his domain, there was certainly no comparison. Tiger was demanding, tough and unyielding, a terrifying Tabby determined to get his own way by fur means or foul. At large on the domus, he was an ever-present threat to Susie and to Nimrod, and the gardeners had their work cut out to prevent serious cat fights. An early-warning system *par excellence* they reigned supreme, to protect both cats in their charge by security and vigilance from a tiresome intruder.

Frustrated, Tiger accordingly directed his fury elsewhere. Outward appearance made him seem a friendly cat – a kitty to caress. Tail high he greeted all he met, to rub and purr for their attention. But once indulged, he rolled over to claw and bite the unwary with a savage yowl.

Downing soon came to know Tiger for what he was; and Porters warned tourists to exercise caution when approached. From far and wide, visitors thronged the Colleges; and if most were well behaved and welcome in Chapel, Hall and grounds, some were trying and intrusive. They trailed litter, infringed privacy, walked on lawns and trespassed in gardens. They could also complain; and when an American *grande Dame* received a 'Tiger bite', crisis came for the cats in the shape of blame to be levied on all.

The Governing Body would have to meet, and time itself stand still with endless twitter. How fortunate then that, even before an agenda item was prepared, the Dean received good news. An architect's letter advised that builders had finally completed restoration of his country house, and well satisfied that their work was up to standard, Peter Bicknell wrote to approve the move.

Although Downing had been a rich experience, I was well rid of the College. Saved from Tiger's talons, I was catapulted off to Landbeach with the minimum of fuss. A Corgi reunion was nigh; and even if my fifth life had ended, there was no need for a stressful soliloquy from a cat about to meet real dogs.

6

'A crow flying north from Cambridge takes the line of the old Roman road, the Akeman Street of the antiquarians. Five miles along this track the level of the land drops to form the first fields of the old fens in the little parish of Landbeach, which straddle the boundary between upland and fen, south of the Isle of Ely.'

In such well-chosen words, local historian Jack Ravensdale introduced Landbeach in his *Domesday Inheritance*. A picture-book village of less than a thousand inhabitants, Landbeach provided an ideal rural retreat for a Cambridge don and his extended family. A residential University, Cambridge insisted that Faculty reside within a five-mile radius of Great St Mary's; and if the Council of the Senate duly approved the village location, the family found their new home all the more acceptable.

Although accurately a Regency property, North Farm's elegant exterior bore testimony to the way classical Georgian design endured in the English countryside. Unique in the region, and to Dr Ravensdale 'a gem of domestic architecture', the house faced the old Village Green across a half-moon drive; it was set well back from the road behind two towering pines and a huge holly bush. Superb symmetry gave the front elevation all the balance style required. Centrally placed, the fine front doorway – an entrance impressive for its white pediment and pilastered surround – was flanked by tall shuttered sash-windows on the ground floor. Ranged across the first floor, attractive and uniform with period glazing bars, three further windows were well placed and in line. And above, as if to grace the façade of a dignified doll's house, ran deep overhanging eaves, a wide soffit and dentils. A serious cap of blue-grey, the slate roof toned in well with many a serried row of Cambridgeshires, the mellow-yellow bricks that, under solid chimney stacks serene on the skyline, afforded weight and mass to substantial real estate. As if to please a puss cat too, moulded in a garish red, lion heads placed at intervals stared out from the soffit board.

What scope North Farm offered the whole family; and nobody was more excited by the Landbeach move than Master Nimrod. So recently honoured with a proper name, his singular status as a Siamese prince now promoted him to be a country squire. For here was a residence comparable in every way to what he had enjoyed in the Catswolds, or for that matter even to his birthplace in those far-off Essex days. Accommodation inside the house was spacious – roomy but never rambling. And outside, beyond the back door, beckoned buildings to delight a cat's heart: storehouses; a loose box; and above all, a two-bay timber-framed thatched barn. Set in two and a half acres, here was territory fit for a prince, another 'true wilderness' Nimrod could make his own.

In his enthusiasm, my Obliger has taken the very meows from my mouth! It was, I recall, the furriest fun to frolic about the walled garden of my Landbeach Estate, and particularly to see the

Corgis again. Jane and Bess returned from Coln sometime after I had settled in, so I was able to welcome them to North Farm.

They seemed to remember me well; and Bess in particular, if still under her mother's watchful eye, sought to be my special friend. We raced around the garden together, and when I climbed the Walnut tree, she would even wait for me to take in the view.

Eureka! What a relief it was to discover Corgis that took to a cat as much as he warmed to them! Any frosty behaviour thawed out within five minutes of their reunion, and when the dogs were walked, Nimrod pranced along behind, round the paddock and even across the fields in the open country beyond. From time to time, the cat did his best to provoke Bess, but not once did she snap or retaliate as had been feared. For when they left Coln, Mary had warned Grace of the young bitch's foxy fame as a boarder. It was a reputation villagers referred to as 'kittying', because in their midst was a Corgi well known to chase every cat that came in sight.

At North Farm other priorities appealed, and led on by Nimrod, Bess became a busybody. She ferreted through discarded agricultural machinery, poked about old ploughs and generally nosed her way around every inch of the barn base. As she did so too, Nimrod climbed aloft to look down on his companion from the wooden beams that framed the old structure. And when interest prompted him to mew, Bess exchanged snuffling for a stare – an intelligent upward glance to focus her friend in a frame that made her ready to heed his command. What a portrait it proved: canine intelligence at its best; alert ears; and the white ivory of a Corgi grin to heighten and endorse the strength of a striking chest necklace in fox and black. Once the runt of Jane's litter, steady growth had transformed Bess into a rare tri-colour damsel for Nimrod to approve. That he did so, both Peter and Grace were clear, however much they knew that as a true cat, he usually preferred the solitary life. It was a choice Nimrod decided to prove in a strategy of barn exploration; and a policy he was to pursue at the highest level.

Snow had fallen – the first of the Winter, and the first in Nimrod's own experience. Warmed by the Aga, kitchen comfort confined the dogs to a large basket both enjoyed. But intrigued by the eerie noise of frosty flakes falling against the windows, the cat waited by the back door. Already fed, he was impatient for a kitty cruise, and none too pleased when Grace said "NO!" But if principles of proud, responsible housekeeping lay behind her decision – slush must soil the tiles and, thawed, would certainly muddy newly-laid carpets throughout the house – Peter and Jenny longed to witness a new Siamese experience: his first sight of snow!

"Silly cat, you'll catch your death," came the colloquial from Grace, herself very much the cold mortal. And to support her stance, she unfastened the top of the kitchen's stable door just enough to draw a sleety draught inside. Alerted to action stations at once, the snow flurry that arrived was nothing compared to the fur flurry that left as the cat seized his chance to leap and claw his way outside. He landed on an icy terrace, a slippery carpet of two or three inches, and clearly confused, began to flick and sample the snow with his paw. With splendid disdain, excitement spluttered into doubt at the damp until evident dissent demanded he shake the flakes from his fur and skid off to seek shelter in the barn.

A gaunt reminder of the key role it played as part of a working farm, the two-bay barn was a mere shadow of its former self. Once assertive and secure, its long thatched roof loomed at right angles to provide a picturesque landmark for those who journeyed the roads from Cottenham and Ely. But now ruined after farming years of arable inactivity and structural neglect, large areas of thatch had slipped away. In short, with timbers exposed to the elements, the very skeleton was at risk of rot. Doubtless crashed by a cart and unrepaired, broken hinges prevented central-door closure on one side; and wind and weather did the rest to bring disorder within and play havoc without. Although access was unrestricted because of the broken door, a cautious Nimrod stopped in his tracks to face the cavernous entrance, fully aware that foes could lurk in the shadows. But blown behind by the blast of an icy blizzard, he had to take cover, and in leopard mode again climbed aloft to claim a lair.

Falling fast, the snow had begun to drift, and to escape the full force of the wind, the cat sought a draught-free perch and settled on a cross-beam summit. High in a loft, he'd found a good landing, a vantage-point snuggery; and ideally placed for safety and surveillance, stared out through the gloom.

With sound and scent to guide him, Nimrod knew full well he had company and was not alone. Yet however frustrated by the squeaks of rodents below, he was far more fascinated with a figure that faced him on the far side of the barn. Motionless for a moment, it was a feathered form that shared his interest in mice; and with a sudden descent, silently secured prey and returned to feed. Eaten head down with a gulp, only a tail lingered to disappear with a shake. And soon a second swoop repeated the exercise as if to grant encore. Nimrod could scarcely take in what he saw, and found himself mesmerized by the owl's silence, speed and skill. He could not take his eyes off the bird, and though he found it hard to face a stare himself, became as observant as any birdwatcher. Paws tucked under, he settled in for the night and steadfastly ignored search parties that came to tempt him down. Not to be seduced by the rattle of dishes below, he remained on high, undeterred and ready to hide away from any human who dared curtail so valuable an opportunity for the further education of a cat.

At first light, Peter and Grace extended the search. With snow tracks obscured by further falls, clues were hard to find and only surface bird prints in evidence. Moreover, when all outbuildings were securely locked, the barn alone offered hiding places for a cat determined to spend a night out – a night not so much on the tiles as under what was left of the thatch. Sure enough too, soft yowls came from precisely that direction, a kind of penitent plea and apology for any trouble caused. Relieved and in good heart despite her sleepless night, Grace was the first to spot the cat seated high above on a cross beam. When she called, Nimrod rose and stretched with a yawn – but when she beckoned and banged his dish, a pensive puss showed little interest and barely returned a downward glance. Undaunted, Grace continued to coax the cat; and in turn Peter tried to suggest that even a Siamese prince might prefer a place on earth to any such refuge on a rafter. All proved to no avail, however, and though Nimrod eventually compromised his dignity with a partial descent, he took good care to remain untouched and well out of reach. No ladder they possessed could get to his eyrie, and the offer of a platform on high household steps to help him drop down was met by the snub of rapid ascent.

Crestfallen and short of time, Grace went to get breakfast, and Peter was left to ponder the plight of his puss. There must be good reason for such obstinacy: the cat was not marooned and certainly had the courage to come down. By this time too, even the most stubborn pet had to be cold and hungry, so what caused Nimrod to stand firm, to dig in his claws and nail Siamese colours to a beam?

In the hope of a simple solution, Peter began to investigate the barn interior, convinced that somehow careful scrutiny must shed light on the problem. He was correct, and on the ground towards the back of the bay opposite Nimrod's attic – ground whitened with bird lime – he found pellets scattered at random. Regurgitated and in that sense repulsive, such tightly-packed parcels and undigested rodent remains provided certain evidence of owls. Nimrod's motive was clear: he had remained at his post to face down a Barn Owl, and would not withdraw. To retreat was out of the question, and the proverbial curiosity that killed cats simply had to be set aside. Glad that Nimrod had not encountered a tougher species, Peter did his best to encourage him on Siamese terms. Happy that he had at least found the cat, he was in a mood to mimic;

and wonder of wonders the 'prrroow' he mouthed from one end of the barn echoed back from the other. Tongue in cheek, so to state, he kept up the cry until clawhold by clawhold, at times in reverse, Nimrod came down.

With a scent and a rub, the cat curled in and out of Peter's legs, delighted that he had been missed. His loss had registered, but whatever its effect, a best friend should know that unfinished business lay ahead. And before his Obliger could caress, let alone recover the cat, Nimrod fled off again. This time, with a mischievous flick of his tail, he raced to the far end of the barn, leapt up to a beam and literally tore his way towards the owl. Almost an action replay of his Corpus Christi exploit on the Master's garden wall, experience stood him in good stead and helped him stand the strain. Wood yielded to claws better than bricks and masonry, and progress was fast and good. The nodding spectre seemed to be asleep, and Nimrod counted on surprise to get a better view. What a mistake! For, talons extended in a stoop, the owl dived at the cat and with hardly a sound flew off to roost where Nimrod had spent the night. Their stations reversed, stalemate set in. Puss-cat prattle – that snarl of Siamese swear words – likewise failed to expel the ghostly presence from the barn. So honours even, perhaps it was time for tactical withdrawal?

Cold, irritated and not a little disgruntled, Peter went off to breakfast while the cat mulled over his next move. Surprisingly warm for December, bright sun not only relayed magic to the icy garden but also began a general thaw. Watery rivulets dripped from shrubs and plants, and fully exposed to the glare, melt water began to stream

from the barn's thatched roof. With no guttering to direct the flow, it plunged to the ground, in some places puddling the perimeter, and in others lying unseen, a hidden menace of moisture.

Their circulation and spirits restored – the fuel of hot coffee and a traditional English breakfast to combat the cold – Peter and Grace returned to their task. With a long enough ladder, they proposed to climb up and claim the cat, secure him in the travelling basket, and bring their coveted prize back to earth. Peter would scale and Grace steady the ladder. Both planned to wear protective gloves. With a couple of working farms nearby too, neighbours would be sure to lend appropriate means. So much for Plan A: Plan B was to call the Fire Brigade!

Before any such action, however, the would-be rescue party went to check key dimensions in the barn. If any borrowed ladder – particularly a double, heavy with extension – could not reach the highest beam, they would carry their burden in vain, and appear fools to new neighbours. But as matters transpired, there was no need to bother about such mundane affairs. For on entry to the barn, they witnessed pure drama.

It was drama played out at the highest level too. For with a paw pointed towards the far bay, a fur trapeze artist seemed ready to cross an imaginary wire. Nimrod would thus surprise the feathered spectator that stared back his glare. His jaws juddered, and his teeth stuttered as if for a kill. Twice his size with arched back and thrashing tail, Nimrod's fury provoked the owl; and with a screech on the wing, it came full tilt to threaten the cat. The bird did not attack, but staged a fly-past and spectacular swoop. And that was enough, for, bewildered by the owl's last-second swerve, a hissing Nimrod leapt from the beam to avoid collision, and clung to a broken weather-board on the garden side of the barn. It had been a near miss, and in shock, the frightened cat forced his way through a broken panel to survive in fresh air. From there he fell to land on a lean-to below the barn – the snowy slope of a large Victorian greenhouse. If he came to no harm – the feline frame, agile and flexible with built-in protection from muscles barely bounced! – he went on to perform a ski-jump worthy of Olympic marks. Under pressure from his fall too, melted ice on the glass started a slide, and as Nimrod's weight added momentum, Peter and Grace were entertained by an impressive toboggan run that ended in a human safety net. For, determined to catch his cat this time, a devoted disciple came to the rescue. By leaps and bounds through slush and snow – and more by luck than judgement – Peter held Nimrod tight just as the cat careered towards a deep drift.

Their mission accomplished at last, it was a trio that returned to the house in very different moods. For if Peter was triumphant and Grace relieved, Nimrod was stressed, cold and weary. The alpine adventurer had courted disaster, and over more coffee, the conversation centred on owls. While Grace cuddled the cat, and an a kind-hearted Jenny came in to give more t.l.c., Peter began to tease Nimrod: "You must learn the simplest colour code," he said, "and learn the difference between brown and white!"

An amateur ornithologist, he knew that, when cornered, all raptors constitute risk; and that Brown or Tawny owls can be particularly aggressive. His close boyhood friend had been blinded by a Tawny attack, and robust bruisers in bone and talon were a force to reckon with. Light-weight by contrast, Barn Owls are all feathers, supremely designed for silence.

107

"Thanks for the lecture!" said Jenny in jest. "Natural history makes a welcome change from Luther!"

Her father was quick to remind her that the good Dr Martinus knew a lot about birds; and Grace intervened with a glance at the clock.

"Just look at the time … you promised to drive me to Ely market, and we must away."

Ende gut, alles gut: all's well that ends well in fact. Nimrod had survived another crisis; and when the family went out to shop, the cat soon made himself comfortable in the Corgi basket with Bess for company.

What a fuss about nothing! To hear them all talk, folk might imagine I had actually lost a sixth life!

Nor am I colour blind – just fascinated by owls. In the Catswolds, Grey Cat had taught me to respect them, but never pointed one out, fur to feather so to say. No small wonder that I found myself mesmerized by that staring, white ghost in the barn. From afar it seemed like a cat – 'chat-huant' in French I'm told – but I couldn't get near enough for a proper view until it flew at me. And as we cats well know, discretion is the better part of valour so it was time to depart! And back inside, with Bess – now almost a Corgi partner – for extra warmth, I'll sleep and dream awhile. As my Obliger has already written, I think I will really like North Farm, and only hope I can stay here in a territory that is precisely the 'true wilderness' I have sought all my young life. It certainly seems to offer every scope – even to a discerning Siamese like me.

7

Decisions, decisions – all crowd in with a move. And after the owl crisis, none more important than the fate of the barn. Peter and Grace had to face facts: North Farm barn had had its day. Restoration would cost thousands, and even if funds could be raised, such monies could be put to better use in other ways. So application for demolition went to the District Council; and once inspection confirmed the structure to be unsafe, permission came through for work to proceed.

At first sight, the task seemed straightforward. Hire a man with a JCB and secure the services of an experienced farm labourer. Then, cap and gown exchanged for hard hat and overalls, Peter could at least try to direct operations. Grace suggested local labour, and instead of thumbing *Yellow Pages* to let her fingers 'do the walking', sent Peter to call on neighbours and seek advice. It turned out to be a brainwave, and introduced them to the Moores.

In truth it was reintroduction, for when a well-known Landbeach rogue had tried to flog a worn-out motor-mower, Bill Moore came over with a warning – buyer beware and all that! Semi-retired as a farm foreman, Bill lived with his wife across the Green. Locals through and through, they made a lovely couple, and the newcomers found them helpful, shrewd and homely in every way. Maud made jam; in season too, Bill sold fruit from his allotment. And with a shared interest in gardening, both wondered what plans were afoot for North Farm. Enjoying a 'jaw', Bill made the first move.

"What'll you do with that barn," he asked, "if yer don't mind me asking? Them folk as just left 'ad plans … schemes of the daughter … plans for a fashion house or summat… Maud knows!"

Replying at once, Peter told Bill that a decision had already been made:

"I'm sad to say it's coming down," he said. "We don't need a huge warehouse for a couple of mowers, and plan to open up the garden."

The old man appeared well pleased with the news, and it seemed an ideal opportunity to ask for his help. Peter again:

"I know little of horticulture, and if you could spare me some time, I'd value your experience."

The conversation paused, but not for long:

"If all's well," came Bill's reply, "I think I can let you have some hours. Me broad beans are already in, and me taters are chitting well. P'raps I'll have space after a week or so. But yer'll need machinery ter bring 'er down! And if yer don't mind me telling yer – and I can manage to ask 'im – Nick Lock's yer man. 'e lives up the lane and 'as 'is own JCB."

Peter was delighted: he told Bill to go ahead; and it wasn't long before terms were agreed and work began in earnest. In many respects, it was a sorry task to remove such a landmark from the village scene, and many were sad to see the old barn go. Made aware of the approaching catastrophe, one neighbour even turned to religion for solace: "Pull down your barns and build greater," he advised. It was a brave attempt to overlay sorrow with mirth, but did not disguise the facts of Landbeach life. Once entirely an agricultural community, the village was to suffer yet another blow and lose more of its rural identity.

Nevertheless, to the dismay of eager speculators, ready and waiting in the wings for any prospect of turning country into town, no development was envisaged. This time no raw estate would demean the local scene – but precisely the sort of expansion a farming community must welcome to entrench rural roots. A kind of 'Gardeners' World' was on the way!

When doomsday eventually arrived, Grace secured all pets in the kitchen, her task to make tea for the men. After loud barks of disapproval, obedient Corgis kept to their basket leaving Nimrod to spy from the window. When the thatch fell, and filth clouded the sky, his wrinkled nose scented the air. And when the whole structure shook, alert Siamese ears twitched at the sound. It was his signal that beams would soon crash to the ground. Outside it was hard and thirsty work, and when Bill came in for tea, he met the cat and shared 'dockey' – some cheese from a sandwich or two. Partial to cheese, Nimrod took to the old man at once; and permission duly granted, he allowed Bill to chuck him under the chin.

"Fine cat you've got there, Sir – 'as 'e settled?"

"He's certainly settled into your sandwiches!" It was Grace who replied, at once offering to replenish Bill's cheese.

"Thank you no Ma'am – I'll save up for me dinner. Maud cooks midday, an I'll need to 'ave room!"

By this time, Nimrod had decided to settle, and when work was about to resume, Bill had to disturb the cat. He did so with care, and held out a semi-recumbent puss for Grace to nurse.

"A good rest'll do 'im good," he said, "with all this row 'e needs 'is sleep!"

Highly amused, Grace capped the countryman's jest with a joke of her own:

"May be, Mr Moore, you've heard that sleep deprivation can kill," she said. "Well if it's true, let me tell you that that cat has no such worry!" And placing Nimrod on a cushion, she left a sleepy-headed Siamese to his thoughts as the men returned to their labours.

I'm not sure that I like sarcasm – whatever humans have to say, we cats find it a poor form of fur wit. But I suppose Grace meant well; and with my Obliger, she certainly does me proud at North Farm with nice warm places to sleep and a good varied diet to eat. I particularly like the way all the family now use my name. It's: "Morning, Nimrod" to greet the day; and: "Night, night, Nimrod" when we go to sleep. When they go out too, it's: "Bye, bye, Nimrod" and: "Hi, Nimrod" immediately they return. Quite right, for all puss cats long to be noticed. Feeding time helps true friendship, and my Obliger strengthens our bond over meals with: "Here you are, Nimrod"; and after a rub and a stroke or two: "Eat it up, Nimrod, it's lovely!"

Outside too, I have plenty of company, and need only be alone when that's my choice. Since the barn came down, Peter seems possessed of a gardening frenzy! Bill comes across several times a week and we all work away with a will.

As far as any human can grasp the feline for *work*, I imagine Nimrod saw himself as our foreman, a kind of 'Kitty-Cat Clerk of the Works'! When Bill helped me to repair the garden wall and lay a terrace round the house, Nimrod was certain to assist. He would dig in the sand, sit on the slabs, and leave his monogram on wet cement – the paw mark of a distinguished fur mason. Puddles he also proscribed, and knew that crazy paving needed special care. For to avoid dips and hollows collecting rain, a spirit-level had to be used. It was work that required knees-on precision and every care; and if the two men took turns to correct any rise or fall in the expanding mosaic, a shoulder-weight burden descended. Nimrod had come to double-check operations the Siamese way; and workers must learn that, to be effective, real on-board scrutiny had to be transferred.

When Spring came and brought warmer weather and longer days for exploration, the cat turned his attention to the paddock – a 'true wilderness' beyond the walled garden where he loved to roam at will. At the mercy of wind and rain, it had been a wild haven – but there Grace planned a kitchen garden and Peter hoped to plant shrubs and trees. With the voice of experience, however, Bill held that little could flourish without a wind break. And so Dood Elwood was introduced, and came to plough a furrow right round the boundary – a furrow deep enough to take the roots of young trees and ease the back-breaking toil of transplantation.

A day's hard work did the trick, and after Bill and Dood had left, Peter and Grace went to view the site. Taking stock, they tried to picture the paddock under cultivation and sort out between themselves the best use of such space. Never one to be left out of a family conference, and with definite views of her own on garden design, Jenny came along too. With her were Nimrod and the Corgis, arrivals that made any serious discussion short lived. For if Jane was intrigued by piles of disturbed soil lying banked up beside the boundary, and Bess sniffed her way along the top of the mound, Nimrod explored the trench. There were severed roots of blackthorn and hawthorn to paw; pebbles to prod; and briar spurs to avoid. Almost in bloodhound mode on top of the earthen heap, Bess trundled through trailing brambles, and with excited yaps yelled out finds of rabbit fur impaled on thorns. In no time at all, the serious human conference had become an animal circus. What began as sane discussion now seemed almost insane, the animals taking over to enjoy an amazing rough and tumble. Spring fever and their unique spirit of adventure were combined in a new kind of game – a cross between trench warfare and tumble tots! And to the confusion of their three spectators, this was played out with gusto until it was time to go in.

Once Spring had fully sprung, feathered life took over

and reigned from dawn till dusk. Early birdsong roused the village, and the Song Thrush /Blackbird choir that led the daily dawn chorus caught Nimrod's imagination and made him a keen observer. He remembered that Grey Cat had found birds boring, but did not share her view. The Barn Owl incident surely proved how interesting feathered predators could be – even that they could teach cats a thing or two.

Hurrah! My Obliger has got the message! Birds can be fascinating, and I was genuinely sorry for that owl when the barn came down. He lost both shelter and a good food supply when the rats left to make other runs, and must have found hunting more difficult. Perhaps he got new lodgings next door in the barn at Old Beach Farm? But I wouldn't know how you'd cope with a roof of corrugated iron when you've been used to thatch? And the screeching noise of Starlings is enough to drive even a 'Screech Owl' to distraction! Perhaps I'll help and take up bird watching for a change? There are Starlings to see on the roof of the cottage next door.

How true! Taking its name from a medieval charter – the record of an open-field system – *Skachbow* predated North Farm. The spare seventeenth-century cottage faced the Cottenham turn, its thin form well back from the road at right-angles to Green End. Dilapidated, with a thatched ridge needing repair, it offered ideal nesting sites, and had particular appeal to a flock of unruly Starlings. Irrepressible survivors, these greedy birds holed up in the roof; and far worse than House Sparrows, actually advertised their rowdy behaviour. They were brazen beyond belief, and whereas other species tried to nest in secret,

Starlings boasted residence from the roof tops. In defiance, they piped out invitations for all to hear almost as if to court disaster, and treat it with contempt. What an offer for a cat – an offer Nimrod decided to accept. So marrying opportunism with aggression, he wended his way and set off for Skachbow. What was in his mind can only be imagined; but the North Farm family faced a day of uncertainty, another anxious night, and the beginnings of discord with a next-door neighbour.

With her customary bark, Bess announced the post lady's arrival, and Grace collected the mail. This was usually taken from the letter-box in the hall; but with a registered packet to sign for, she gave Rowena coffee at the back of the house; and when Rowena left to continue the round, the Corgis saw her off, leaving Nimrod on the terrace.

There, busily engaged in one of many sporadic washing sessions that crowd a cat's day, he was rudely interrupted by squawking from Skachbow and went to investigate. He confronted a Starling sortie, and clawed his way into action. Bully birds clamoured irritation, and stealing from rivals caused petulant screams in response. It was noise without end – the deafening din of hungry youngsters pestering parents from hidden nests. Humans may moan about parrots – but their mimicry cannot compare with the tiresome way Starlings annoy cats, and Nimrod determined to lodge a Siamese protest. Low on the ground and hidden by a thick yew hedge, he fixed his gaze on a tall tree, a leafy ash that overshadowed the cottage.

Tuning in to harsh sounds with not a little fury, the cat soon secured sharp focus on the source. From several directions, and at regular intervals, parent Starlings landed high in the ash and used the tree as a staging post. They then descended to the cottage roof and fed their young. Birds arrived, and birds departed; and as they passed in the air between tree and thatch, or thatch and tree (for this was frequent two-way traffic), they yelled at their rivals. No mere greeting but voluble swearing, the pitch was high – as high as crops crammed with food allowed – and received loud backing from nestlings eagerly awaiting another nibble.

Bewildered and temporarily confused, the cat was unsure of his next move. Strategy alone could win the day, and like a Siamese Duke of Plaza Toro, Nimrod planned away behind the lines. He would be seen if he climbed the tree; but crouching along with stealth, he could surely reach the cottage without being observed. Once there too, he could take further stock of the situation and give his mind – a Siamese mind as brimful of genius as any Goon Show – to deciding what next!

It worked, and wriggling his way through a row of early carrots, he drew up to Skachbow undetected. If only that tail kept still, surprise would remain on his side; and if it didn't, surely busy Starlings would believe that those vegetable tops were just swaying in the breeze? By the back door stood a water butt; and from there, with a bound and a leap, he'd be on the roof ready for battle. His past came to mind – no experience was ever wasted on Nimrod – and purposeful climbing for a kill was in sight again. But just as the skirmish was about to begin, the cat noticed an open door. Was there another way? What a ploy it would be to startle the Starlings by getting at them from *inside* the cottage! Such a surprise attack must leave them speechless!

The cat did not pause, and entered Skachbow without delay. Two doors led off a tiny vestibule – one to what was obviously a kitchen; the other to a small front room. His choice was clear too, lamb chops on the kitchen table shouting welcome! What a diversion! Someone evidently knew his preference, for with good red meat on offer, who would waste time sampling feathered fowl, let alone scrawny Starlings? But no sooner had Nimrod helped himself to the choicest chop than, in tremulous tones, a human voice shouted: *"THIEF!"* Shutting the back door behind her, an angry woman had appeared. Resenting his presence, she even tried to revoke her hospitality. But that was not to be,

and firmly clenching the chop between his teeth, Nimrod
rapidly withdrew from the table. Showing the woman two
clean pairs of paws, he raced for the front room; and there
he was quick to hide, for with the window shut, the cat
had nowhere to go.

The speed of the whole operation shocked his pursuer. She had never laid eyes on Nimrod, and feared that a half-starved stray might attack. The cat was cornered, and the woman took time to collect a saucepan and a broom before following the thief. It made good sense to startle such a fur rogue and hope he would change direction to leave her cottage without further ado. But Nimrod found it easier to scoot up the chimney instead. After all, there was no cosy glow in the hearth, and once he had discovered a ledge above the grate, it was a simple matter to lever himself up the flue where found a higher ledge at the base of the smoke-stack. In a neglected unswept chimney, it was a grimy business; but seated on his ledge, Nimrod made the best of a bad job and tucked into his plunder. As he did so, he was accompanied, for from above and down below, a musical interlude ensued. From above, throat warbling from the Starlings echoed in the stack; and from below, the clatter of broom handle on saucepan could be heard – a rare cacophony! The unsuspecting birds had been deceived, and the indignant householder confused. For to both parties the cat was well out of sight and had, quite simply, vanished. Left to himself, moreover, Nimrod became drowsy. All that excitement had made him sleepy; and having finished his snack, he deserved a good rest. So he settled down on his shelf and slept, exhausted and alone like a Kingsley water baby wearied by work in the chimney.

Meanwhile, next door at North Farm, Peter, Grace and Jenny were concerned. It seemed that their puss was up to his tricks again. He had missed his usual afternoon siesta, and could not be found. Peter searched the garden and toured the paddock with Bess; Grace checked the house; and

Jenny telephoned neighbours and left messages about her loss. It was an anxious time, and the family were depressed with neither sightings nor returned calls to comfort and give them heart. A long sleepless night followed – a night spent in very different ways. For if only fitful slumber came to the folk at North Farm, flat out in the chimney next door, Nimrod enjoyed a beauty sleep that had rarely been better. Bess tended to snore, and free from such disturbance he made the most of his retreat at least until a screaming dawn chorus broke the spell.

Events then began to move; and they moved fast. Wide awake and ready to go, Nimrod applied himself with his usual single-mindedness. He'd come to Skachbow to sort out Starlings, and fully intended to finish the job. Yesterday he had given way to diversion; but that was now past, and with a new day came new opportunities. Well within range at last, the birds were unaware of his presence; and however steep the climb, their young were confined, tightly crammed in the untidy nest that blocked the flue. At the top of a tunnel, it remained out of reach. Moreover, when masonry lining the chimney became dislodged as he clawed his way to the light, the Starlings were shocked, and the cat fell to the bottom of the shaft in a cloud of soot. The front room was empty, and the door closed. But through the smoggy gloom, an open window gradually came into view and presented a grimy escapologist with another chance. It was just the opportunity he needed to do a second disappearing act. In short, Nimrod saw it as a shrewdly-planned exit all staged beyond the ken of the cottage's long-suffering resident! For although she had wisely left an open window to clear the sooty atmosphere, the householder was elsewhere when the cat made his getaway, an act he performed well enough without her knowledge. When he returned home, Jane and Bess hardly recognized Nimrod as a colleague. They were ready for their morning walk, and demanded to know how even a brown Siamese could come to be *black*.

Although I was naturally glad to be back, the day was not at all what I'd hoped for. First of all, I had to face that colour-code question again. It had not been long since my Obliger had told me to distinguish brown and white; and now the Corgis were fussing about brown and black! I think Bess was jealous that I'd become black all over when she was herself merely patched! Secondly, I had a wash and brush-up to face.

What a business! Still, on balance, it was just as well that a bath from Grace restored my full feline splendour. For thirdly, that woman came round to complain. How did she know that I had called at her wretched cottage? Why should a Siamese squire demean himself so? And even if her hunch was correct, what a mean trick to play on a guest. Anyone knows that an open door and a table laid invites visitors in to a meal. Some meal too when you're chased away from the table!

By now she must have discovered that I had at least the good grace to sweep that grimy old chimney; and she should be reminded that I did it for nothing!

WAH TAH NAH SIAM to put up with such treatment from a human!

❧

Memory gives life real meaning; and to the animal kingdom memory is of the utmost importance. Elephants (we are told) never forget; and nor do cats. Yet to deduce from this that humiliated animals go out of their way to wreak vengeance on oppressors must be set aside as *simpliste* – or in pseudo Gilbertian language 'speculation most extreme'.

Only humankind descends to such retaliation, and can even be capable of waging war to revenge a wrong or demand blood for blood. In marked contrast, animals rarely feud. Rather do they observe long-established rules they find acceptable – rules of seniority, precedence and territory. Crisis and predation apart, their squabbles hardly ever rankle. This makes deference the order of any day, for it takes a really serious confrontation to end in death.

It can therefore have been only mere coincidence that, soon after stalemate at Skachbow, Nimrod encountered another hen from next door. This time he did so in company with the Corgis. Rusted chicken-wire had long been holed; and in many places great gaps had opened up. Free to come and go at will, it followed that poultry was truly *free range* and chickens more at home in North Farm paddock than when restricted in their own Skachbow run. Regular trespassers, they took pleasure pecking their way through Bill's vegetable plot, and were particularly partial to fresh young lettuce. Once caught, of course, they were duly returned to their run; but 'ere long, to the old man's fury, another invasion of feathered fowls was underway.

Enough is as good as a feast; and whether she had just such a feast in mind or no, it was Jane who decided to help. Proud of her pedigree as a Pembroke cattle dog, she never shirked duty. To Peter's surprise, she had once rounded up grazing sheep near a Cheltenham golf course; and with such a claim to fame, hens were fair game. How dare they feed on Bill's vegetables and generally infringe her very own territorial rights!

Nimrod had not been consulted. Bemused at first, he was not one to concentrate his mind on wayward old hens. But when Bess chose to help her mother round up a regular offender, he decided to join in the fun. He'd show them that even an emotional orphan could prove his worth; and hunting in a pack with firm friends, he cornered a pullet in the greenhouse and let Jane make her kill. The Corgis showed little interest in the corpse; they were duly scolded, and this time the body was not returned. Folk can count after all; and rapid repairs were soon undertaken – shades of *Chicken Run* – to prevent further loss. As for Nimrod, he took a quiet pride in being Siamese.

It was time for the Cuckoo to call, a time of year when Bill was busy with his broad beans. He'd set seed long since; and in his own Green End garden nurtured young plants with tender care. Rewarded with an early crop, he was well pleased; and when Nimrod chose to cross the road to meet Maud, he was also rewarded with a cat she described as 'a most distinguished visitor'. A lady's maid, Maud had spent her early life in service, and knew quality when she saw it – quality at county level. Retired and in her late sixties, she had not only given her life to Bill and their son Roy, but was also given to hospitality. Visitors were welcomed with open arms, and Nimrod was no exception, receiving not only a fuss, but also the splendid cheese squares he so relished. What a *rendezvous!*

For No 38 was immediately opposite North Farm, ideally placed for dropping in. So in no time at all a Siamese social whirl began. Unobserved, Nimrod would run across the front lawn and hide under the holly tree. There he would pause to take in the traffic. He hated vibration; the rumbling of heavy sugar-beet lorries, and the racket of farm tractors to-ing and fro-ing from fields outside the village. When the coast was clear, he would race over the road, vault the little gate, and arrive in Bill's garden. Laid out at the side of his cottage – a semi-detached building directly fronting the footpath – the plot was screened from the street with a neat yew hedge. And in the centre of a well-kept lawn, Maud's white magnolia had pride of place. Beyond stood a small greenhouse and around it a carefully-weeded area devoted to vegetables; and outside the back door a colourful cottage garden where the little old lady loved to tend her roses. Beyond again too – behind a boundary wired to contain cattle – lay open meadowland. Once part of the Manor of the Chamberlains, its trees, banks and ditches – for flood defence was necessary on low-lying land so close to the Fens – composed a rare medieval landscape the whole village had fought to preserve.

In Landbeach, friends and acquaintances came to the back door when making social calls, and careful to follow local custom, Nimrod did likewise. When at home, Maud would receive the cat in her porch way; and there, as often as not, he purred away admiring her skill with flowers or tempting cuisine. He knew by instinct that she was good at household management and needed no extra help, particularly a prodding paw.

Far better to stretch out in the warm sunshine and wait until – Maud's floral tribute or Bill's midday meal prepared

– it was titbit time. Then, after a tasty snack and a moment or two spent on wiping his whiskers and cleaning his chin, Nimrod would take his leave and return to North Farm on a roundabout route through the fields.

It was Bill who first made the family aware that 'a certain cat' patrolled his garden, snacked with Maud, and went a-rambling in the fields on the far side of the road. He warned of danger from fast cars, and of drivers who, with the 30 mph de-restriction sign in sight, accelerated at high speed as they made for the Cottenham turn. Without due care, neither man nor beast nor bird stood a chance and accidents were known to be rising. Taken aback, Peter thanked Bill for his trouble. He would heed such a timely word in the ear, and do what he could to keep Nimrod to the territory the cat knew at the back of the house. In any case, with such a vast open space at his disposal – acres of garden, woodland and field – why ever would any sensible creature wish to roam more widely?

If Peter had posed a question, he did not really expect a reply. But responding at once in a whisper – shamefaced and full of regret – the old man muttered the word '*cheese*':

"It is the *cheese*, Sir," he said, "…'e loves 'is *cheese*; and I've told Maud to lay off …"

And together they laughed, at the same time being clear that, as far as possible, Nimrod should be kept under close observation. After all, if Maud withheld her treats, the cat could well get bored and stay at home. While the men conversed, the cat was very much at home dozing by the Aga as they chatted over mugs of hot tea. Comfortably composed on a cushion, he was in a world of his own and intended to stay that way for as long as possible. He may well have been under discussion, but if he kept his head well down, he surely wouldn't be disturbed and left in peace in the Land of Nod.

≈≈

Seedtime and harvest highlighted the farming year. They were also peak periods for those who laboured on the land, weeks when sheer pressure of work stood in the way of any holiday arrangements and prevented labourers taking even the briefest leave. Similarly with daily milking duties to meet, Bill's cow men rarely had a break. But having taken time for his own leave, the farmer insisted that his foreman went away when times were slack. He prized it almost as much as crop rotation, and Bill readily agreed. With Maud's blessing they saved up and travelled by coach far and wide the length and breadth of the land. A yearly cycle too, it was one they continued in retirement, usually taking time away in the middle of May. And when Nimrod chose to call again, the Moores were not at home.

It is said that absence makes the heart grow fonder; and although the sentiment may hold good for some humans, cats not only find it meaningless but also frustrating. In truth, Nimrod felt well nigh betrayed when, on a sunny day in May [19 May, for it was St Dunstan's day], he went for a visit to find the door closed and no-one there to receive him. The very thought of it made him feel worse. For had he not gone to endless trouble making good his escape from North Farm? First of all, knowing his Obliger to be an affectionate observer who didn't miss much where his cat was concerned, he waited until Peter was out. Secondly, aware that after attending to fur elegance in yet another careful grooming session, Grace would not miss him but go off to wash and replace his brush and comb in the pet cupboard. Thirdly, he knew she would then attend to the Corgis – an ideal doggy distraction providing an astute cat like himself just the chance he wanted to slip away unnoticed. Clearly, what humans call 'a window of opportunity' was at hand for him to escape. For although a puss is more precise – imagine the indignity of squeezing through the kitchen window when you have the physique to vault that stable door again! – did it matter? He'd gained his freedom – even got away without his collar because Grace had forgotten to fit the wretched thing again – and was away on another of his vanishing acts. For once Grace had time to seek him out she'd soon be in despair, for rather like *Macavity* he'd simply not be there.

In fact, crossing the Green at speed, Nimrod raced over the road. But then, after all those careful plans, his high hopes were dashed. The cottage was deserted; Maud was nowhere to be seen; and with no cheesy treat in store, the cat suffered a sad anticlimax.

He paused to take a sporadic wash, and after a moment checking his whiskers, decided it was time to move on. And so he padded down the path beside Maud's rose bed, and went under the wire at the end of the garden into the field beyond. What fun it was to be there, to find himself half-hidden in lush, long meadow grass! Pasture green and puss-cat *yellow – dents-de-lions* in fact! – enough feline flowers (dandelions!) to make his Siamese heart swell with pride. As for his pointed face – what a portrait it posed for the discerning. A dark chocolate brown head was most impressive when topped with alert black ears; and that did not even mention the staring eyes of vivid blue which gave Nimrod such a mask of mischief. For here was a cat at the ready, fully prepared to take on any trouble in sight. But apart from the pleasant spring breeze that whispered and rippled its way through the long grass, nothing seemed to move. Nothing, that is, apart from Nimrod himself; and he moved rather like a perched owl. After his recent experience, he resented the comparison however much he knew it held good. For there he was, sitting tall and on the look out, his slowly-swivelling head turning by degrees to take in the view and focus on the far and middle distance. Fully equipped with ambush power, a lone warrior had arrived, ready and longing to hunt. Yet only the grass stirred, its false alarm attracting the cat's attention for the briefest moment before being dismissed as a playful diversion an inexperienced kitten might just deign to paw.

Brooding birds – however well camouflaged on hidden nests – rarely sit tight for long once they detect the presence of predators. And although she had not been observed, the hen Pheasant was decidedly unnerved by another brown study near at hand.

So the deeply musing Nimrod almost jumped out of his fur coat when the feathered fowl literally exploded into flight within yards of him. Worse, it rocketed off in a way that warned the whole field to beware. The cat cursed his luck – so near and yet so far! And the shock made him move. It was clearly not his afternoon, and if he had been inclined to wait for the first rabbits to emerge from their burrows, dusk was still some time away. Better then by far to return to North Farm and his own feeding bowl. It was beginning to rain too, and there was certainly no point in getting wet without good reason. Accordingly, Nimrod retraced his steps through the field until he reached Bill's garden.

At that stage speculation took over, for it was difficult to record precisely what happened next. Yet certain events came, and they came thick and fast. Thick because as Nimrod ducked under the wire to grip Maud's rose bed with his paws, breezy blasts – gusts just like those he'd found so fascinating when they'd rippled the meadow grass – turned round in eddies to tickle his tail. Stimulated by such an exciting sensation, he started to run, and did so at top speed round and round the magnolia in the middle of the little cottage lawn. Fast was surely the word too, for at much the same time he spotted two Collared Doves courting on the green sward just over the road at the front of North Farm. Cooing away, the cock wooed the hen with many a bow and a scrape. Obsessed by their mating ritual, and grounded with nothing but sex in view, the doves had not noticed the cat; and the sharp-witted Siamese knew that such perfect prey was there for the taking. A quick charge must fell the pigeons before they took off; and he put on a spurt intending to cut them down before they could fly away. Caught unawares – *in flagrante delicto* – the birds would neither know what had hit them nor live to tell the tale. Or so the cat mused as he headed full tilt for the road. But the Siamese streak was ill-timed, and at the very moment he leapt off the grass verge outside the Moore's garden gate, Nimrod collided with a fast car entering the village from Cottenham.

CRASH! BANG! His very world had come to an end. Light turned to darkness; and he bounced back unconscious to lie in a crumpled heap by the wayside. If the car slowed, the driver did not stop but blundered on regardless. Made without a care for the village or any life that lived there, the journey was a regular rat-run through Landbeach, a mere detail in the daily diary of a commuter. How fortunate then that, although hardly en route from Jerusalem to Jericho, a good Samaritan woman came along to save the day. The lady in question – three cheers for careful women drivers! – had witnessed the accident, and promptly braked to stop. Just like the Samaritan of old she was full of compassion; and if binding wounds with oil and wine did not come into her equation of care, she certainly offered just what the emergency demanded: immediate ambulance service. Knowing a lot about cats, she realized that a glancing blow of the kind she had seen need not have killed the unfortunate creature. There was no bleeding in evidence, and the cat might survive if treated for shock. So without delay, she deftly wrapped the victim in a blanket and took him straight to the Cambridge University Vet. School.

By the time Nimrod's rescuer had driven to the Madingley Road, slight stirring in the blanket indicated that the cat had regained consciousness and was far from dead. As she entered the Vet. School she even heard a pitiful mew, a cry she regarded as confirmation of her lay diagnosis that the cat was suffering severe concussion at the very least. But that was not her problem, and handing the burden over to experts, the modest heroine withdrew, her name unknown to this day. Moreover, the vote of grateful thanks that for ever remains her due has also to be shared with the Vet. School. For that Faculty of Cambridge University has never been an A & E reception centre, and it was only selfless service from animal lovers present at the time who saw fit to accept the casualty. Sick pets have to be treated by Vets in practice; and if they reach the Vet. School they only do so in much the way patients referred by their General Practitioners get to hospital. This the Samaritan lady saviour did not know; nor did the Vet. School let her down.

Once admitted the cat was duly checked over with every care. He was checked for internal injuries, for broken bones, and for internal contusions. He had suffered severe clinical shock; and although bruised and decidedly miserable, was just as surely unbowed. After receiving a pain-killing injection, he found himself in a quiet, darkened recovery cage where he spent the night. Under constant observation, he was checked at regular intervals, and evidently made the most of quietness in the small hours to sleep off his nightmare experience. For bright and early next morning, a perky, purring presence was to be found rubbing back and forth along the cage as Master Nimrod announced to all with ears to hear that he was ready and waiting to go home!

But where on earth was home? The cat had no collar, and his owner was difficult to identify. Only a place name had been registered when he was brought in – the village of Landbeach. *Landbeach?* Was not that where Polly, one of the Vets, lived? If so, she might just have some idea of whom to contact? And so it was that on the morning after another of those nights before – hours of haunting anxiety and no sleep at all for Peter, Grace or Jenny! – telephoned inquiry brought good news to North Farm. A shocked Siamese cat had been handed into the University's Vet School and…

"According to a member of our staff, he is the only such feline known to live in your village. Does he by any chance belong to you? If so, he is, even now, clamouring to be collected!"

And collected he was without delay, a chastened cat with his own tale to tell:

Moonstruck in a wire cage, I found myself confused by the sheer rush of events. For the vision of doves that clouded my mind ended with a loud bang. I was left in the dark, and passed out for what seemed an age in the blackest of nights.

When I managed to see again, strange sounds crackled in my ears and I felt terribly sore. I gather I must have been travelling to the Vet. But quite unlike my other visits, this time I was alone and very worried because, with my Obliger absent, there was nobody I knew to comfort me. A full examination followed, and although sad, stressed and insecure, I was well looked after, an injection helping me to sleep. My memory is still something of a blur, but I feel a little more relaxed this morning and seem to be on the way to recovery. I shall need a lot of peace and quiet to restore my mental balance, for I've been given to understand that complete disaster nearly came my way and I'm lucky to survive. Be that as it may, we cats have a relaxed outlook, and I want readers to know that all Siamese look on the bright side of life!

8

NIMROD was not the only member of the North Farm family to be stressed by the road-accident experience. For although there was nothing new about the cat going missing again, when inquiries were made this time a number of neighbours passed on rumours of road kill. No one had actually witnessed anything untoward; yet somehow word had gone round that an unknown car had stopped by Green End verge in the late afternoon. It seemed that the driver had got out carrying a blanket; rapidly returned with a bundle; and driven off without delay. Putting a brave face on such news, Peter put the incident down to Pheasant poaching. But as time went by, Grace convinced herself that Nimrod could well have been involved if only by reason of his continuing absence. The more she pondered the situation too, the more she feared the worst, becoming almost numbed with sadness. Accordingly, there was not only much rejoicing when news of Siamese survival came down the wire, but Nimrod also received a fine old fuss when Peter brought the cat home from the Vet. School.

HOME is just the word I'd use too! For after losing my liberty and freedom yet again – I think my Obliger has recorded the crash as the seventh crisis of my life – I really needed my home. I had certainly been well looked after by the Vets who treated me. But at North Farm I knew I was loved. And although still

shattered and sore, I let them all know how much I wanted to
return their affection. I particularly loved my Obliger because it
was he who came to collect me. So when he lifted me out of my
travelling basket – he did it with the greatest care lest my sore
fur limbs were jarred – I did my very best to arch my back and,
with a rub and the loudest purring I could muster, express deep
gratitude to let him know how much I appreciated such kindness
from my servant.

During the weeks that followed, Nimrod evidently
enjoyed peace and quiet, preferring to settle down as an
inside cat for the first time since his kittenhood in Essex
and Kent. To start with, almost as if welcoming a change
in life style, he soon made the most of family routine and
the support services a shrewd cat can always find on offer.
Peter was an early riser, and when he dutifully brought
Grace 'wake-up' tea in bed, Nimrod expected a saucer
of milk. It was then time for Grace to go down and get
breakfast, and as she made her preparations, a fur *sous-chef*
eagerly watched the proceedings. He did so from a book-
shelf by the Aga, and became a kind of back-up bookend
that not only supported Mrs Beeton's *Complete Household
Management*, but also drowned the splutter of frying bacon
and eggs with Siamese culinary advice. And that was only
the start, for when serious meal preparation got underway
later in the day, rarely had a cat shown such interest in *haute
cuisine*. Good food was never taken for granted: it had to
be received with gratitude. And Nimrod well knew that
even the best cooks valued encouragement from those they
served with long hours of selfless devotion in the kitchen.
There were, moreover, ample rewards on hand for a cat
prepared to mew a running commentary on recipes and

be ready to sample and taste acceptable ingredients, or any kind of fare a cook's generosity might hand down.

Needless to state too, for recuperation to be real, rest had to receive priority; and in his puss-cat convalescence, Nimrod made much of the idle life. Decidedly a connoisseur of creature comforts, he followed his Obliger everywhere to find resting places all over the house. In the study, he chose to sit on Peter's knee, tapping typewriter keys whenever the mood took him. The fur imprint of oriental paws simply had to assist early-morning correspondence: it would also help his Obliger to hurry upstairs again. For once admitted to Peter's dressing room, the cat never lost an opportunity to stretch out in the jersey drawer. There

he would sink into the wealth of woollens kept at the bottom of a wardrobe, sorting and scenting his way through neatly-folded pullovers until he was able to savour selected sweaters to his satisfaction and settle down. So while Peter shaved and dressed, Nimrod kneaded and purred in pusscat ecstasy. And if his Obliger soon hurried off to Cambridge to meet the demands of a heavy teaching day, a relaxed Siamese warmed woollens in a drawer and did so to his heart's content.

At lunch time, a rattling dish summoned the cat downstairs again; and after a snack he usually followed Grace round the garden before returning to bask in the sun on a sofa by the drawing room window. In Autumn and Winter too, the daily round was much the same except that, when the warmth of the sun was exchanged for a cosy glow in the hearth, Nimrod settled on a stool near the fireside. Revelling in the heat of burning logs, he whiled many a hour away gazing spellbound at the flickering flames. Moreover as the charred embers were consumed before his staring blue eyes, it was as if their changing patterns radiated *joie de vivre,* and despite ordeal by fire, conveyed the warm satisfaction of survival.

In short, although unquestionably stressed and worried when he first returned to North Farm after his frightening experience, it was not long before the cat regained most of his old confidence. Curiously too, Nimrod even became interested in cars, showing particular fascination for his Obliger's *Sirocco* when Peter parked it by the back gate. Attracted by warmth again, the cat spread himself out to emboss the bonnet whenever he could, and did so with lofty defiance. Was this a survivor's challenge to vehicles in general, a challenge mewed forth with pride? "Why hurt me? I've done nothing to you!" Any attempt to get into his mindset can only be speculative, but laying down terms with solemnity and style, Nimrod left muddy monograms on the paintwork – marks of triumphant survival clearly visible for all to behold!

The cat's paw marks were certainly noted when Polly's husband called at North Farm to ask a favour:

"I see Nimrod continues to flourish," he commented to Grace as she opened the front door.

"However did you guess? And how kind of you to inquire," came her reply. She had recognized the visitor and invited him in.

"I spotted his signature on the *Sirocco* as I came down the drive, and although I'm here on a doggy errand, Polly will want to know that her patient has bounced back to life!"

"Well almost so," said Grace, "but do come and see for yourself."

And together they entered the drawing room where Nimrod, comfortably crouched on a stool with paws tucked under, reigned in Siamese splendour by the fire. He greeted them with a bored yawn; and after a blink or two dozed back into another of those siestas that, increasing in series, now framed his pattern of life.

The visitor chose not to disturb the cat and came to the point at once. He hoped the Brooks would spare time to record some doggy reflections for an animal programme he had in mind for the BBC. Barbara Woodhouse was already involved, together with various professionals Polly had herself recruited from the veterinary world.

Grace was quick to react:

"We are not professionals," she spluttered, "just the merest amateurs who love Corgis, and … (almost by way of a postscript granted the various shocks she had suffered of late) … the *odd cat!*"

Her visitor smiled and took the point:

"Just what I'd hoped for," he said. "*Lay* input from pet lovers. I would like to agree a time when you and your Peter can ponder some questions and let me record your answers as part of a survey broadcast on keeping dogs."

Grace agreed; diaries were consulted; and a date arranged when the recording duly went ahead.

⋙⋘

Months later, the whole family tuned into a programme *Radio Times* entitled '*Man's Best Friend: The Whole Morality of Pet Keeping*'. Written and devised by Peter Taylor, the broadcast was presented by Clive Jacobs, and produced by David Winter. If no-one initially recognized their own voice, Bess clearly knew her bark, and a mystified Nimrod seemed intrigued by a curious echo that made his ears twitch. For when 'talking to animals' came under discussion, Peter had recorded the Corgi's reaction to the word 'AMTRAK'. Newly returned from a lecture tour in the US of A, he had had a conversation with Grace and Jenny comparing British Rail with America's Amtrak, and both were highly amused when Bess butted in! Word emphasis often prompted the little dog to interrupt – she was invariably conscious of human conversation – and with seven woofs and a growl, she went on the air recording her barks for the Beeb!

Duly noting his best friend's notoriety, Nimrod gave the dog a condescending stare, a studied glance prompting mirth all round as the broadcast continued. But like Queen Victoria, even a royal Corgi like Bess would not have been amused had she taken heed of Barbara Woodhouse and her attempt to justify the 'de-barking of dogs.'

"De-barking can save the lives of many dogs," she argued. "It softens the bark and keeps peace with neighbours. A tiny nick in the vocal chord is all that's involved, so a dog can still express itself, and enjoys a hearty meal after six or seven hours when it comes round… of course there's scar tissue, but it's a perfectly painless operation. I don't recommend it, but it saves lives."

Running for thirty minutes, the programme ranged widely. Experts held forth on the place of animals in human society; and whether owners thought their pets had souls. Were animals necessary for human self-esteem? And were they good for sociability in the lives of men and women? Was it right to make a hobby of keeping a pet – a dog, a cat or a budgie? And when a high percentage of tortoises and small birds died in transit, how could such trade be justified? Often the focus of everyday conversation, were animals, as some humans hoped, destined for immortality? As for the vast financial outlay in feeding pets, on what grounds could it be justified when millions of the world's children were starving? Finally too, the broadcast posed a basic question – a supreme challenge all pet lovers have to face, namely: <u>Are humans really capable of being best friends to any animal?</u>

Provocative in every way, the broadcast was no sentimental survey. Pet ownership was portrayed as a demanding responsibility – the commitment of regular day-to-day routines. Properly observed it imposes the duty of care – the solemn change to consider any and every creature involved for the long haul of a lifetime.

Miaow to you too! How long-winded can humans be? And however can they devote a whole BBC programme to dogs? Admittedly it was fun to hear Bess bark on cue, but better by far to suggest listeners look out for feline friends and seek the love of cats! We don't need constant attention and much prefer to keep our independence. All pets should learn to exploit their minders; and because many deprived humans rely on animal companionship in lonely lives, we owe them no apology for demanding food and comfort. But dogs are always underfoot! They show no initiative unless they want to go 'walkies'! In marked contrast, felines know how best to use freedom and – unless rats, owls, cars or wayward hens intervene – come and go with comparative safety. Always remember that you cannot have true joy without a little pain.

I dote on my Obliger and seek his affection all the more since he came to get me after that car crash. I don't like rivals, and as a general rule too, if I am not given love and petting when I need it, I'll race away and get up to mischief until I'm missed! For it's sheer heaven to stage a come back; be forgiven again; and enjoy a regular fur fuss!

141

After his holiday in Scotland, Bill was eager to work again, and twice a week he came over to garden at North Farm. Years before, in his Manor Farm days, he had taught Dood Elwood to plough; and the deep furrow Dood made at Bill's suggestion proved ideal as a way to ease planting the paddock perimeter. Sixty balsam poplars were spaced along the trench; and in time they not only scented the air, but began to shield the field from prevailing winds. Within the now secluded square – an area well over an acre – other trees were planted, and Peter went to Scotland where a good friend allowed him to fill an estate car with a generous load of young larch. Bill and Maud had themselves found a potted pine on holiday; so in no time at all it seemed as if a mini-arboretum had been transplanted from Dumfries to Landbeach.

Grace was delighted with her vegetable plot; and Bill as keen to make the area productive as Peter was to enclose it behind a hedge of beechen green. For his part, Nimrod preferred the hedge recalling, as he did from Grey Cat's lecture course in his Catswold days, that hedges provide superb wildlife corridors and soon become happy hunting grounds for canny cats. He also discovered tunnels used by long-tailed field mice. Criss-crossing the roots of two mature walnut trees, these were so near the surface that, combining careful observation with a ready claw, an alert cat could usually claim a quick snack.

In and out of season then, Peter, Grace and Bill cultivated and cared for North Farm's paddock, vegetable allotment, and gardens. The paddock was a paddock no more. It had been transformed into a well-stocked plantation containing a fine range of specimen trees and shrubs. Of these, most were European larch, young trees comprising a fine copse of deciduous conifers glowing bright green in Spring, and gradually fading to autumnal golden-yellow when their needles were shed before Winter. Such seasonal change could have brought a barren look to the copse; but care was taken to intermingle evergreen conifers with the larch, and these came into their own in Winter. Of particular interest and well placed for their appeal were: a fine specimen of the blue cedar; a dominant green abies already standing tall; a young spruce superbly layered with a growing crinoline of blue branches; a freely-fanning turret of yellow cyprus; a dense cryptomeria of deep green that turned to burnished bronze in Autumn; an island-bed of skyrocket juniper, its blue-grey finial flanked by golden thujas; and a contrasting isle where rose a weeping cedar between golden 'Irish' yews. A garden arranged in 'rooms' sustains interest and is never boring. And here in the far distance, a vista of oak and maple reached out to the boundary where the former paddock frayed into fields beyond, and where Peter had plans for a gazebo.

Hedged in by closely-clipped green beechlings, the kitchen garden enjoyed a russet frame throughout the winter months. Wind protection gave Grace full scope to use good fen soil to best advantage; and building on his long experience, Bill's hard work harvested a full range of vegetables for the house. With broccoli, beans, beetroot, cabbage, carrots, lettuce, peas, potatoes, radish, spinach, sweet corn, swede and turnip as mainstays, they also had success with asparagus, artichokes and a number of aromatic herbs.

Then there was the garden itself, a good half acre of borders where shrubs and perennials flourished. Its clunch wall with unusual brick stringing not only gave privacy but also lent a period atmosphere; and here much mature planting by the previous owners had survived. Thoughtful selection ensured good colour through the seasons: well-sited and south-facing, a fine old garrya was covered with grey-green catkins as early as late January; mahonia, 'witch hazel' and forsythia radiated different shades of yellow in late March and early April; a showy pink and white magnolia flowered in late April; crab and double Japanese cherry blossom blushed shocking pink in May; philadelphus scented June evenings with orange blossom; a range of potentilla glowed white, yellow and orange from June to the end of September; candyfloss 'tamarisks' came in July; red lycesteria in August; a sky-blue ceanothus began to break in September – October; a rich cotoneaster fanned out scarlet berries later in the Autumn; and 'winter' jasmine not only brought up the rear but, frosts permitting, warmed hearts with pin points of yellow right through to Spring.

Prroow! Should readers think my Obliger has described North Farm Gardens in too much detail – and even added such a measure of artistic verisimilitude to his narrative as to make it bald, unconvincing and irrelevant to my life's story, they should know my views. First of all, the old paddock was where I originally pranced about almost as soon as I arrived to live in Landbeach.

My paws were regularly refreshed with the early-morning ritual of striding through long dewy grass. And when the trees matured, several of them served as my scratching posts. Peter forgot to mention the silver birch. I certainly made the most of the way they yielded to my touch, not only sharpening my claws, but also amusing me as their paper-thin bark peeled away to flutter in the wind.

Secondly, I had my own views about that vegetable plot. For there I not only felt it my duty to keep stray chickens from next door at bay, but also my responsibility to scare off scavenging pigeons. Both were as determined to decimate any delicacies that caught their greedy eyes as I was resolved to chase them away from territory that belonged to Bess and myself. Those who tilled the soil clearly had their rights, but so did we; and we often wondered why Grace and Bill shooed us off their allotment when we were busily tracking down trespassers! I suppose they disliked the way I rolled over on warm ground in hot weather; and I never could grasp why it was they chose to spoil a perfect spot for sunbathing by sowing seeds. When it was warm enough for an open-air siesta, those threads of black cotton were really a bore – restricting and unhelpful. To settle down properly, you simply had to paw them up. Although Bess often got herself tangled in trip wires, together we set about removing them and did a good job as demolition experts.

Thirdly, readers ought to know what I thought about the walled garden; for whereas, once planted, the old paddock became my true wilderness, I found the formality of the back garden altogether enchanting for Siamese seclusion. All cats prize colour for camouflage when hunting, but only the most elegant felines know about tone and colour contrast. And among the bushes and perennials North Farm offered in the shrubbery and herbaceous borders, I know I made a purrfect picture. Why else did Grace disturb my privacy with her camera? I preferred the solitude of peering out from under the trailing garrya; or surveying the scene from the security of jungled jasmine. But even if discerning artists invariably scorn such exposures as 'chocolate-box studies', I think Siamese colouring provides the perfect contrast with white magnolia; just as sparkling blue eyes add an extra dimension to pink tamarisk. And let those who would accuse me of vanity know that we Siamese have always taken pride in our appearance.

What a caterwaul! But in the circumstances it would be unfair to criticize Nimrod and instead rejoice that, having by now recuperated from his near disaster, it was time to record the return of the cat's old confidence. Back with a vengeance, such confidence gave him strength to beat the bounds of his extensive territory with new vigour. Among the trees he would lie in wait for squirrels only to return frustrated when outwitted by their speed and sheer agility. He also kept a look out for woodpeckers. Many luscious worms wriggled away below the turf in grassy glades, and foraging for such a meal, one unfortunate bird actually fell victim to the cat. A 'yaffle' (a country name for the Green Woodpecker) drilling aloft in the trees was one thing; but such a large bird probing about on the ground quite another. And quick to take advantage, there actually came a day when Nimrod proudly presented his latest conquest at the back door. He would also play havoc with Wood Pigeons raiding the vegetable garden. The beech-hedge avenues provided perfect cover, and many a slow take-off delivered a full quota of fat pests whose feathers fluttered down to decorate the beds.

Then too, by regular patrols on top of the wall, he would use the garden to best advantage. In season, crumbling clunch provided many a crevice-hide-away for nesting birds, and several species caught the cat's eye. Flirting Robins asked for trouble, and proved sadly vulnerable when fighting over territory. However much they revelled in the wall too, the sheer speed of adult titmice usually prevented their becoming prey. But baby Blue Tits were another matter; and although many survived because their parents struggled to rear large broods, numerous tiny tots met a pawsome fate. In turn, Nimrod found Spotted Flycatchers especially diverting. Always on the look out for insects, and perched on strategic vantage points, they were a pleasure to watch and would intrigue the cat for hours on end. What a pity then that, once these summer migrants chose to nest, their untidy structures were not difficult to find. Spilling out from precarious ledges in the clunch, they were barely disguised and soon became a Siamese heart's delight. For in the garden, Nimrod would rarely miss a trick, on one occasion even making play with Pheasant eggs. Discovered in the herbaceous border, he rolled several from the scrape the hen had made as if 'knuckling down' to a game with giant shooter marbles.

And games were certainly high on his agenda in 'May Week'. For it was then that Peter and Grace hosted croquet parties. Once *Tripos* – Cambridge Finals – was over, third-year undergraduates enjoyed blissful days of leisure before class lists were published and their degree results known. They punted to Grantchester; prepared for the 'May Balls' held in June; and generally made the most of what remained of their 'Varsity' life. Faced with the tedium of marking scripts – not to mention interminable examiners' meetings – dons had a very different deal. But once student assessment was over, most tutors entertained deserving pupils; and they did so either in College or in domestic retreats of their own.

After the summer house was built, North Farm provided an ideal venue for a number of reasons. First of all, Grace readily extended the hospitality of a real home to young people otherwise accustomed to live in College or cope with lonely lodgings. With a real interest in entertaining, she used 'May Week' as an opportunity to extend 'Fork Suppers' – like those regularly held for Downing's Chapel Choir – by inviting pupils who attended her husband's University Seminar and Supervision classes. And Peter highlighted the event by claiming a sixteenth-century context. Annually – when holding forth on Luther's reformation – he made his lecture audience aware that, although he could not for a single moment compete with Saxony's Frederick the Wise, and that Elector's vast treasury of holy relics, he prized a singular shrine of his own: the field in which Erasmus kept his horse! When lecture-hall laughter subsided, explanation followed. For William Gonnell, schoolmaster of Landbeach, looked after Erasmus's steed when the celebrated humanist came to teach Greek at Queens' College. Convinced that the schoolhouse was once sited where North Farm came to stand, local historian Jack Ravensdale argued that Gonnell cared for the horse, and kept a mount ready for Erasmus to flee away when plague came to Cambridge. Correspondence existed to prove the point, and this Peter shared with his students. So at garden parties they were interested to see plaques composed (appropriately in Greek and Latin) and set in the wall to commemorate the fact that 'Here Erasmus grazed his horse.'

Needless to state, Nimrod was always ready to display himself on such gala occasions. A cat with the conceit of Cicero, he would view the game with interest as croquet went ahead on the lawn below; for seated on the top step of an apron flight below the plaques, he lent dignity to the whole proceeding. Having been taught to lay bricks by Cecil Strype, Peter had built a summer house on the old barn base – and this provided a perfect pavilion for the use of croquet players and spectators. And when it was time for refreshments, Nimrod would process across the lawn and, rubbing round any hoops along the way, present himself for a fuss before demanding any *canapés* in sight. In frisky mood too, there were times when he pawed the wooden balls; but finding them too heavy to please, he preferred the ping-pong ball one undergraduate produced. This, to the surprise of spectators, he actually pursued through hoops; but when wooden mallets were rattled and waived in tribute, Bess barked her protest and the cat fled off into the shrubbery, taking a bow with his tail all curved.

It followed that conversation centred on cats as much as it did on croquet. Since Victorian times, both had been fashionable in Cambridge life; but if most undergraduates knew their College cared for a cat, few of them knew the rules of croquet.

"It's my very first game," said one.

"But you must have seen dons hard at play on the Fellows' lawn," another replied.

"And what an unkind game it can be," said a Girton girl whose boy friend had just driven her ball off pitch, managing with a mean mallet 'to croquet' his main opponent.

So when Nimrod returned from the bushes to adorn the summer house table with a pleading look in his eyes, the gossip naturally turned to cats.

"Surely, he's not still hungry?" queried a Trinity man. "If he had to sample meals in Hall, he'd jolly soon realize how you spoil him here!"

Grace intervened and, sympathizing with those who had to face institutional food, joked about Downing where students were all too often confronted with chicken on the menu. "So much has this been the case," she said, "that of late the JCR voted to register complaints about the Steward's bulk-buying of *twenty-legged hens!*"

When a Petrean chose to commiserate, students from other Colleges half-expected a patronizing manner, for Peterhouse had a University-wide reputation for good food.

Instead, however, he turned the conversation back to Nimrod and asked Peter if he knew about Mr Kenney and the cats he kept in College.

"Most certainly," came his host's reply. "And did you know that when Professor Kenney's entry was published in *Who's Who*, he recorded his *recreations* as 'cats and books'!"

"Well there's a *first!*" interjected another bright spark, all applauding the speed of the rejoinder, hopeful that such good results would soon come their way.

And it was a merry gathering that then rehearsed cat tales galore – a goodly cross-section of young people reminiscing about their family pets. If various remarks were made about the haughty independence of cats, these were soon countered by memories of puss-cat companions and the close comradeship many owed to feline friends. It came as music to Nimrod's ears – a complacent Nimrod who, in their very midst, echoed such music with contented purring of his own.

⧽⧼

September was a busy time in the vegetable garden. The ground had to be cleared for planting spring cabbage; outdoor tomatoes needed to be held at no more than four trusses; courgettes and cucumbers picked; and main-crop potatoes lifted. Taking particular care of the 'taters', Bill followed a well-tried system he had long made his own. Convinced that 'jestics' were the best variety, he set about lifting his crop towards the end of the month rather than in October. Early frosts were rare in East Anglia, but Bill would take no risks and harvested with the utmost care. He hardly ever damaged a tuber; gave them all good time to dry; and set about constructing a clamp. The traditional way to give the best protection, it was like building a small wigwam of straw wound around a pyramid of potatoes before covering the crop with a good layer of soil. Conveniently placed for the house, he sited the structure by a path that ran parallel to the garden wall; and there it stood proudly displaying a straw chimney to allow ventilation. For more immediate use too, Bill filled several bags with surplus tubers, and these he wheeled to store in the loose box on a specially-made barrow, slatted, sideless and ideal for the purpose.

Ever a supportive spectator, Nimrod did his best to study the proceedings, and did so with his customary attention. So when the odd small spud missed the open sack and fell to the ground, he sprang off the barrow and lent a ready paw to help (or was it to frustrate?) the harvest. Nor was he alone; for while Bill was wheeling the barrow away, and the cat cleaned offending fragments of earth from his whiskers, a Brown Rat appeared from nowhere. Furtive and decidedly undaunted, the wily creature also chose to seize a small potato which it rolled down a gentle incline towards Skachbow's henhouse. There, under the floor, beneath roosting perches and a wall of compartments laying pullets used for their eggs, the thieving rodent had a nest. With others huddled together in a veritable rat retreat, it had lost no time in welcoming Bill's potato wigwam, regarding the nearby store as a private market garden for the colony's especial use. Moreover, once harvesting ended for the day and night fell, a real rat pack set to work, and burrowing through the wigwam, pillaged away with a will.

By the morning, the rodents had certainly made their mark; and when Bill arrived intent on further autumn clearance, Nimrod came along too ready for more fun. But as events soon proved, fun was not to be the order of a very different kind of day. For almost at once, instead of a potato, the cat spotted a thickish tail slithering into a hole in the clamp. In no time at all too, a large rat came out backwards, clinging on to a spud, a hard-earned prize it rolled away in the direction of the hen run. Nimrod blinked: he could hardly believe his eyes. This was nothing if not daylight robbery; and he was witness to a daring theft.

With a covetous look in its eyes, the rat soon returned for more booty. But the rodent's strangely gliding gait came to a rapid halt when Nimrod came into view.

Cornered by the cat, the cunning creature reared up ready to fight, baring stained yellow teeth with a loud squeal. Altogether unnerved, a spitting, swearing Nimrod took up the challenge at once. Without as much as a pause to tiptoe around or ponder tactics in a battle plan, his claws shot out and gripped the brown body in a tight vice. Then, with a swift lunge of his jaw, the cat neatly nipped the foe with a well-placed blow at the back of the neck. Precise timing and fine physique had triumphed: the rat's body relaxed, slumped forward, and after a brief sequence of terminal shivers, lay still on the ground.

Attracted by the racket, both Bill and Peter had been present to watch the fight, Bill standing at the ready with his spade raised.

"Yer never knows with them critters," he said. "When caught unawares, they're real savage and battle away like nobody's business to protect young 'uns."

"Quite an experience," replied Peter. "I must admit I was worried by the way Nimrod put himself at risk."

At this both men looked first at the dead rat, then at a somewhat subdued Siamese.

And while Bill collected the corpse with his spade, Peter went to pet the puss. After such a dramatic incident, Nimrod appeared surprisingly nonchalant: he hardly arched his back, and seemed almost unmoved by his lead role in the brave act Bill and Peter had witnessed. Bill again:

"Well there's a cool customer, an' no mistake! If yer don't mind me telling yer, Sir, you've a cat in a million there. It takes a real good cat ter stand up ter a rat like that un!"

"Even so, Bill," Peter replied, "I think I'll whisk him off to the Vet for a shot or two.

It's about time for his booster anyway. You never know with rats, do you?"

And making a wide gesture in the direction of Skachbow's infamous hen house, he continued: "There are bound to be more rodents where that chap came from; and immunization is the best form of protection!"

⤜⤛⤚

Miaow … Prrrow … Miaow!

To hear them talk, anyone would think I've lost my eighth life! But at least the Vet was pleasant enough. He has a practice in the next village; and when my Obliger took me along to Maple Cottage, Milton, he seemed as caring as all the other Vets who have had me through their capable hands. I can't say I like injections, but you can certainly count on a great deal of fuss after those jabs, and then have a chance to rest in peace while you feel woozy!

As for rats, they seem to be the bane of my life! I'll never forget my first experience of such vermin in Canterbury. Fancy being led on and dumped in a dungeon for a whole night and a day! Then there was that Barn Owl: he taught me a thing or two about rats! Indeed, you could go as far as to say he taught me how best to deal with them; and it was his theory I put into practice in this most recent drama?

They tell me the best Romans longed to engage in gladiatorial combat; and I have at last managed to do just that with human spectators present.

Of course I've always known of my Obliger's pride in me; but to have old Bill on side as well is a real triumph for any Siamese prince!

9

*H*umans aren't the only ones to feel depressed after visiting their surgery for a health check-up! I could hardly believe it when I overheard my Obliger sounding out my survival prospects with a Vet! Anyone would think that I am already in my dotage for they actually discussed my age! Peter seems to have no idea how long we felines can expect to live; and the Vet, indicating that a mightily 'altered' puss like myself could easily make it to seventeen human years, was at least reassuring on that count.

They also mentioned something humans call a 'mid-life crisis' – a condition the Vet suggested my Obliger could spot for himself if he kept a look out for what he described as 'behavioural change'! He warned that the grey hairs he fondled on my ebony muzzle were clear signs of ageing. I was most offended, but calmed down a little when he congratulated me on my sylph-like figure. I shall long treasure the very words he uttered: 'Unlike some cats I see in my surgery,' he told Peter 'Nimrod is in no way obese and should have many more years ahead, if only you can keep him trim!'

Back at North Farm I pondered his words when purring away to myself by the fire. Somehow I feel more sociable, and less inclined to roam. Whereas the human family once had difficulty persuading me it was time to come in for the night, nowadays I make such good use of my favourite sleeping places that I'm hardly ready to go out in the morning! My best friend Bess soon urges me on with a 'Tally Ho!' But as often as not she gets my 'Tally No!' in *reply. I wonder if this can be energy loss? Some times I do feel a bit stiff when I jump; and my Obliger seems to understand. So I welcome the way he lifts me on to the bed, and even helps me up when I seek a siesta in my favourite fireside chair. And now I have difficulty leaping up and over that kitchen stable door, he's actually had a 'cat flap' fitted and will often ease me through it if I let him know I'd like a gentle stroll round the garden.*

In no way did Nimrod become more sedate overnight, yet after that renowned rat fight, those who knew him best began to detect certain changes in his feline outlook on life. He slowed down considerably; rarely took risks; and at long last seemed to develop what could be described as a cattitude of solemn Siamese maturity. And, surprise, surprise, it therefore followed that both Peter and Grace began to enjoy a somewhat simpler routine – even days free from anxiety. For however much their mischievous puss continued to be his old, high-spirited self, he now claimed attention in less demanding ways.

Always a cat to take pride in his distinguished appearance, Nimrod seemed less able to keep himself as spick and span as was once the case, and evidently valued help in grooming. When a pliant young puss, he could reach and clean his extremities with ease; but advancing age made such stretching difficult and regular combing sessions were all the more appreciated. And if he had always been famed for a healthy appetite (only rarely being finicky over his food), to the delight of Bess he now ate much less, and a vigilant Grace had to keep Corgi greed at bay. Rather like humans in a second childhood, the cat preferred to snack a little when the mood took him; and, as if back in kittenhood again, looked to his Obliger for small portions, and fresh helpings, three or four times a day. Above all, it was a great relief to find a reformed Nimrod – a cat disinclined to take off on so many risky ventures. And precisely because he tended not to hunt so much for himself, the puss expected more service at home. After all, if failing powers did not bring their own reward, there was no point in being a pet, and a cat's life was not worth the candle!

Then too, as well as ageing, Nimrod went through a bad patch and had to face frustrations in plenty. The worst of these was the death of his best friend Bess. As far as any feline really dotes on a doggy companion, they had been inseparable ever since being reunited and resident at North Farm. They ate, slept, and walked together, particularly enjoying mad games of tag, racing round and round trees in the copse, and playing hide and seek in long field grass beyond the old paddock. If there were times when Nimrod found Bess a little overpowering – her choice of a perfume obtained by rolling in Pheasant dung did not appeal to the cat – he made allowances. After all, for her part, the little Corgi gave him a wide berth whenever he reeked of cat-mint. Nor did Nimrod approve of Bess's taste in carrion, for the more gamey the corpse she discovered, the more avidly it was consumed. No wonder Grace nicknamed her 'Dustbin'; and though it was undignified for a Siamese prince to indulge in scurrilous name-calling, Nimrod had his own reservations. Not only did he deplore his friend's gluttony, but also frowned on the way Bess wolfed decaying remains at a gulp. A bad habit fraught with danger, he feared it would one day become her downfall, and was proved right when, escaping from the garden, Bess bolted bait set down for rats. The side gate had been left ajar, and the dog seized the chance to forage at Old Beach Farm next door. When she returned soon afterwards, something was clearly amiss. Far from her usual lively self, she had become lethargic, flopping out on the tiled kitchen floor as she struggled to breathe. It was clearly an emergency situation, and Bess was taken to the surgery without delay. Her Vet confirmed a clear case of poisoning: internal bleeding was already underway, and as multiple organ failure was sure to follow, he held out no hope.

The whole family was devastated; and evidently conscious of loss, Nimrod spent several weeks looking for Bess in the many old familiar places she had, with him, made her own. Cats can certainly grieve, and Nimrod seemed to mourn his Corgi companion so much as to make Peter and Grace aware of a void in his life. He had never been close to Jane, but a curious loneliness now brought him closer to Bess's mother almost as if the animals had chosen to find consolation and comfort in one another. So when Jane suffered a stroke only a few months later, and severe paralysis deprived her of any real life, she too was put to sleep to avoid further suffering. Both Corgis were buried near the gazebo at the far end of the old paddock. And there to this day, in a simple cemetery, stand tombstones that, in true Quaker style, duly display the names and dates of the dogs buried there:

BESS   JANE

1971 – 1982   1967 – 1983

≈≈

A further setback confronting an elderly cat came with an unexpected gift for Grace. Very much the dog lover, she had not been allowed a pet in her childhood; and following the loss of both Jane and Bess had felt almost bereft without canine companionship. Regular dog-walking had kept her in close touch with like-minded friends and neighbours in the village; and had also helped her to exercise and lead an active, healthy life. So when Peter surprised her with a Schnauzer for a birthday present, she was overjoyed. The youngster came from a reputable Cheshire breeder, and Grace was as glad as Nimrod that Peter had not gone for a puppy. Instead he had managed to find a dam whose third season lay some months ahead. This he reasoned would not only give the young lady time to settle down in her new home, but also give him time to take her to stud and prepare for a litter at leisure.

Research had taken Peter to Germany from time to time, and there in leisure moments he had come across the breed and found it impressive. Not that North Farm needed either the ever-popular *Mittel Schnauzer* – let alone *Deutschland's* Giant Schnauzer of guard-dog fame! Professional advice suggested a miniature of the breed would be ideal; and recalling Canterbury days (and Corgi Jane's happy event) an energetic young bitch arrived. Well bred and bearing the Kennel Club name 'Buffels, Sweet and Saucy', the miniature was a slate-grey colour, correctly termed 'salt-and-pepper'. She toned in well with the cat; and once he got to know her, Nimrod had to admit he found her breed less boisterous than the late Corgis of blessed memory. And when he overheard Peter recounting the reputation of Schnauzers as 'good ratters', the puss cat warmed to 'Buffels' all the more, however much he deplored the sheer absurdity of such a given name! Needless to state, that wrong was soon righted, Peter suggesting 'Kate' instead, the name of Martin Luther's remarkable wife.

In short, the animals tolerated one another, Nimrod even showing a full measure of long-suffering when Jenny fell for what the cat was amazed to hear her call 'a rescue dog'! Surely if dogs had anything about them, it was their job to rescue humans, not *vice-versa*! And how on earth a peg-legged mongrel could rally to any cause he knew not! Nevertheless, Cassidy (as in 'hop along') came to stay, restoring the animal population to full strength. Yet for the cat, matters went from bad to worse as it was not long before Kate, having been introduced to a husband in Burwell, was delivered of two puppies, Flo and Libby. What a palaver for an ageing Siamese: a vast whelping box took up space in the kitchen; peaceful nights were disturbed caring for the expectant mother; newspapers littered the floor; extra bedding and heating pads appeared; Vets threatened; there seemed to be unending supplies of *dog* food; and too much fuss gave hardly any peace to a cat!

Once weaned and out of their run too, Flo and Libby – puppies very difficult to distinguish and accordingly labelled 'that one' and 'that other' – were awestruck by Nimrod. Indeed, so much was this the case that, whenever the cat appeared, he came in for such undivided attention that he had to remain hidden – in fact to lie doggo! – to have any life of his own. How times had changed since the good old days of Corgi Bess! North Farm was not what it was: no self-respecting cat could possibly put up with so many dogs. Hard times to be sure, but if Nimrod found it bad enough to share his home with such usurpers, he had another surprise in store when the Newells moved to Old Beach Farm and a cat-loving family came to live next door.

Dick and Vida Newell were devoted to cats, and with their son Séan and daughter Ali, presided over a multi-puss household. Whereas their predecessors had little time or liking for pets, the Newells effectively had a cat each, however much it was Dick who cared for felines most of all. Built about the time of the English Civil War, Old Beach Farm was the first brick house in Landbeach. Rising above white limestone foundations pillaged from the medieval manor of Chamberlains, attractive and double-fronted, its pink brickwork rises two storeys high, includes a staircase tower, and boasts fine gables with roofs of mellow tile. Well restored by the Seeley family and offering splendid accommodation, it had become a grand haven for cats, and Nimrod soon learned of four Newell tabbies free to roam in every room.

Thomas was a friendly cat: handsome and well-pat-terned, he sported a striking white waistcoat with match-ing high socks. No cuddle cat, William had a very different character. Impressive by any standards, he had an attractive ocelot coat and startling black-striped cheeks. Then there was Topsy, Thomas's sister. With similar markings to her brother, and well-loved for an affectionate nature, she was, in Dr Newell's meaningful phrase, 'the ultimate cuddle cat.' And last but not least came Oscar, splendidly tiger-striped and as elegant a puss as a tabby can be.

If the Brooks and the Newells quickly established the best of relationships, Nimrod found the presence of so many feline neighbours not a little disturbing. An elderly Siamese prince simply had to frown on English 'moggies', and although the tabbies initially tended to keep to themselves, they gradually encroached on territory Nimrod regarded as his own preserve. It was time for espionage, and whenever opportunities presented themselves, he delighted in spying on the newcomers from afar. When face-to-face confrontation surprised him too, he found it uncomfortable, and tried to vary the timing of prowling routine in order to avoid his neighbours. At the outset, it did not seem to cross his mind that rivals had arrived on the scene. But that condescending Siamese manner got him nowhere, and although he may have kept his pride, he very soon began to lose his empire.

William was the first to invade. An avid rambler, he regularly accompanied Dr Newell when he crossed the fields on bird-watching expeditions. And carefully shadowing the puss from beneath the outposts of North Farm's tree canopy, Nimrod knew he would be no match for such a fursome athlete. Nevertheless, he had no plans to cut and run; and although conscious of a crisis situation, he did his best to pose coyly and stood his ground in the copse.

Topsy's approach was very different, for she did her best to flirt with her exotic new neighbour. Nimrod was the first Siamese she'd been privileged to meet; and although she well knew she must have encroached on his territory, there was just a chance that such a splendid prince would value the services of a devoted mistress and courtier, however changed his personality. At first too, with no sound of a hiss, they indulged the odd sniff. But that was the end of it all; and as if realizing the *actualité*, Nimrod preferred to stare Topsy out until, rejected, exposed and uncomfortable, the little lady withdrew to her own garden.

Brother Thomas also wanted friendship and fun, but chose to pursue that objective in a boisterous way. He voiced his introduction to Nimrod with a chatty miaow, and made a mock charge. What miscalculation! No such move should be chanced in a first encounter! And spotted by a singularly serene Siamese some time before he ambushed Nimrod from behind a bush in the North Farm shrubbery, Thomas's impertinence was rapidly rebuffed. With a yowling growl quite foreign to his vocabulary – no-one in the human family had heard such a noise before! – Thomas was told to keep his distance. In territory terms, this was Nimrod's way of telling Thomas to beware! Elderly Nimrod may have been, and though he well realized he was ultimately no match for a youthful trespasser, he remained a Siamese squire who would not be pushed too far!

At least Dr Newell knew about cats, and when he called at North Farm, Nimrod took an instant liking to Peter's new neighbour. For Dick introduced himself in a properly respectful way; and the cat understood from the start that here was a friend. The men also shared an interest in ornithology, Dr Newell particularly praising the larch plantation where he had not only observed a good range of migrant Warblers, but also heard the twittering refrain of tiny Goldcrests. Apart from birds of course, their conversation naturally turned to cats, and referring to past mischief, Peter hoped that an ageing Nimrod would not make himself a nuisance to the Newell family. Dick was amused, and told Peter that he had already been made aware of the cat's reputation as a thief. Apparently, almost as soon as his family had taken possession of Old Beach Farm, Skachbow's cottager had called in the hope that she could involve the Newells in the life of her village. Duly noting their cats, the lady expressed the pious hope that, unlike the Brooks's Siamese, Newell pussies were not thieves! Although they had yet to be properly acquainted, Dick had at least seen Nimrod for himself; and viewing the cat from his study window he greatly admired what he saw. Ever protective of felines too, he met the accusation with disbelief. It was surely impossible to charge *'that posh cat'* with such misdemeanours? And their new neighbour should learn not to tell tales out of school!

Laughing, the men compared notes about cat behaviour; and while on the subject of light-pawed larceny, Peter learnt about Oscar, the fourth Newell tabby. If ever there was a fur thief, it was Oscar. Sharply-pointed, his very features gave the game away, hinting that here was a pillaging puss always on the look out for any loot in sight. Oscar fondly imagined that if he could not see the person in possession of his quarry, he would not himself be seen. Rather like a Bingo player, the cat kept his eyes well down, and when the time came to pounce, would seize booty at high speed. In fact, all was achieved so fast that, on one celebrated occasion, Oscar actually snatched a guest's chop from her plate with the fork still in it!

Thus the men reminisced, swapping cat tales and the experience of many sightings of rare species they recalled from bird-watching days. And as they did so, fondled and fussed by Peter and Dick in turn, it was as if, eavesdropping on their conversation, Nimrod himself became a 'twitcher', swinging a restless tail from side to side. Lacking in confidence, he might well have to swallow his pride after all and face facts: the time had come when he no longer had strength to face up to the many trials that challenged him in old age. He was outnumbered by both dogs and cats: dogs from North Farm, and cats from Old Beach Farm.

Worse, he had the distinct impression that his much-loved human family, with real distractions of their own, had themselves become too busy to care. Jenny had married and moved away; and one by one her children were brought home to meet and stay with their grandparents. Not long since, Kate's whelping bed had crowded Nimrod out of the kitchen; now, when babies arrived for weekends or on holiday, play pens and walking frames combined to make inside life unbearable for a cat. He had become an exile in his own home; but turning to the best feline initiative he knew, did what he could to solve a real dilemma. So in Spring and Summer he retired to the greenhouse; and there, propped against gardening gloves in an old wooden trug, he found as snug a lying as any old man's care home to while away the evening of his life. And in Autumn and Winter, he took a liking to the utility room where the washing-machine drum provided peaceful seclusion. Cushioned by dirty laundry, it was fine; and safe occupation could usually be guaranteed with a flick of the tail through the open porthole door.

However resilient his response then, Nimrod had to face new endurance tests; and he showed quite remarkable stamina in a determination to survive on his own terms. Although his territory had shrunk, he refused to feel restricted and clearly preferred coexistence to conflict. So when uninvited visitors came knocking on his door, he avoided close contact with other cats. There was no need to lower himself by rubbing shoulders with tabby rivals who might turn round, battle and beat him up. Better by far to use discretion; to revise his empire; establish new frontiers; and avoid indecent squabbling in a cat fight. In any case, with the frequent small meals his Obliger made available for a senior puss, he had less need to take up hunting, and might just as well allow others the use of his territory by letting out roaming rights in order to keep the peace.

Not that Nimrod ever stopped playing the rogue. So much Miss Joan Nash found out to her cost. While 'house-sitting' for her friends the Brooks, she invited her cousin to dinner, planning a meal appropriate to good Australian appetite. From Gawthrops – a respected family butcher in the next village – she had ordered thick cuts of best filet steak, and in her absence, these were left on the kitchen table. But not for long. In consequence, while a certain Siamese feasted on rare red meat in the greenhouse, a changed menu for the 'barbie' obliged Joan to serve Joyce cheese and biscuits on the terrace.

GGrrrooowwll! And why not, I say?

I can't be expected to eat grass; and Grace recently removed her precious spider plant – my favourite meat supplement – to an inaccessible hanging basket in the conservatory. And by

167

taking my revenge on her best friend, I thought I'd get my own back, for Jo is bound to report me when Grace returns. I jolly well hope she does mention the matter too, because it proves that, despite the many catastrophes my Obliger has already mentioned, I am not pussyfooting around and do not intend to give in to usurping Germans, a mongrel dog and those tabby 'moggies'! So when I can't even get near the Aga, and filet steak is so generously left out for me on the kitchen table, it's hardly surprising that I ran off to enjoy it away from the dogs in my own private dining room!

They say History repeats itself – and my paw, grab and run raid was a repeat performance of what I did on my visit to Skachbow during my early period at North Farm. The cottager clearly recalled the incident, and from what I gather still bears such a grudge that she rehearsed the matter as a 'scandal', called me a 'thief', and did her best to blacken my reputation with the good Dr Newell. She's obviously forgotten that I have a black face – jet-black ebony it is, and as hard-wearing and long-lasting as my memory of her antipathy to cats!

I've always hunted for myself and shall continue to do so if I possibly can. I simply must have a stimulating environment to keep sane – so when they accuse me of 'mood swings', let them think again. I've been crowded out by silly little dogs. Bess may have been a dwarf – the literal translation of the Welsh word for CORGI so I'm told – but she was a Giant friend to me, and one I dearly miss.

I miss my Obliger too, and find life on the lonely side without him now that he seems to be away so much. He understands my day-to-day demands more than anyone else, and even went to great trouble installing a special door for me to come and go as I please without the strain of climbing out. Not that I'm decrepit … not quite! In fact, when there's steak on offer, my old bones seem to serve me as well as ever. I'm certainly quite surprised at the athletic prowess possessed by a geriatric puss cat. But after all, as Dr Newell said, I am a 'posh' Siamese; and whether he meant that to be a tribute or mere fur flattery, I shall treasure his words as long as I live.

❦

The fact that Nimrod had noted his Obliger's frequent absence came as no surprise.

Retirement had arrived, and with it the prospect of moving house, sizing down, and lessening the work load of running North Farm. At first the lure of the Lake District beckoned; or would it be more appropriate to contemplate a new life in the less-known, secret kingdom of Northumbria? And what about the sunny South-West – Dorset or even Cornwall? Rural France likewise had much to offer as a peaceful retreat for what evening years remained.

But in the end, the idea of keeping North Farm in the family, and handing down a fine property to the grandsons, presented the perfect solution if only because it would best maintain valued links with Landbeach. And when an early Victorian cottage came up for sale in the village High Street, compromises were reached and plans duly finalized for Peter and Grace to move barely half a mile distant from their old home.

At first, a mere down-the-road removal had many advantages. Compared with departure for destiny in some great unknown, it clearly offered a most attractive solution to domestic life in retirement. Yet although costs were afford-able, regular contact with local friends and neighbours maintained, and all the amenities of a splendid university city like Cambridge kept on side, there was one serious snag: Landbeach High Street had become a busy thor-oughfare and was no place for a free-range Siamese, or any other cat.

And with that fact in mind, the family decided that Nimrod was best left behind at North Farm. After all, many puss-cat pundits believe felines to be more attached to their surroundings than to any human support; and as Nimrod knew Jenny well, and Peter intended to keep his library at the farm, the cat could surely enjoy the best of both worlds? He would be cared for and kept safe in a house and garden he had come to regard as home; and would still be fussed by his Obliger whenever Peter came to work in North Farm study. As events soon proved, how-ever, the solution was not quite as simple as that, and for various reasons matters were far from straightforward when applied to the puss.

To begin with, although Nimrod may have felt secure, he was nevertheless bewildered by such changed circum-stances. A true oriental by character, the Siamese had long shown Peter more dog-like loyalty than most felines afforded their owners; and he evidently missed the regular routines Jenny – as the dedicated mother of young boys – could not hope to follow. Fortunately, on 'M. Day' itself, the cat had chosen to settle down in Peter's den before the van arrived; and with the study declared out of bounds to all removal men, Nimrod apparently revelled there in cloistered calm, sleeping through busy hours of noisy upheaval.

But trauma was still to come, for although the Schnauzer family went ahead to the cottage – Cassidy remaining with Jenny as a pet for the boys – the place Nimrod had to himself he found hard to recognize. For gone were his old favourites – furniture such as his stool, his rug and the sacred sweater drawer in the wardrobe. Instead there were new items to scent; and the ritual of replacing new smells for old was itself an unnerving experience. In similar vein, he found the boys far too attentive, their persistent prodding no boost to morale. To be fussed over was one thing – he was just about prepared to face having his fur forcibly smoothed down by inexperienced youngsters – but to have your coat ruffled up the wrong way quite another matter, altogether deplorable and no support for sartorial elegance whatever!

And being dispossessed was not the only worry to burden Nimrod: he was also obliged to come to terms with devastating routine change. The new management evidently followed different orders of the day, and particularly of the night as far as sleeping arrangements were concerned. Thus at dawn he was not merely shown the door, but made to go out unaccompanied when taking his early morning stroll round the garden. And if breakfast was still next on the agenda, it was no longer the leisurely lounge of a gentleman and his lady, but rather fast-food service with flying lunch-box preparations, bulging bags and backpacks, crashing books and often even rowdy cabaret leading on to what was called 'the school run'. Admittedly peace could then descend, but only in the children's term time. Otherwise chaos continued to reign unless, by good fortune, Peter invaded and, taking his cat with him, spent the rest of the morning in the study. But at lunch time, Nimrod knew that his Obliger usually had to depart, leaving the puss behind to face the rest of a day that invariably reverted to chaos. For Jenny had a young family to care for, and in the pressurized routines of a dedicated mother, peace was a rare commodity. Indeed, quite frankly, there was no peace – at least the kind of peace to warm the fur of an elderly cat. For example, the kitchen had become an unending arena for meal preparation; and what was once a hallowed shrine dispensing choice titbits to a Siamese suppliant, was now a clattering scullery, a deafening den of distraction with its crashing pans, constant echoes of chopping on boards, and the whirring, grinding sounds of blenders and mixing machines.

As for the reception rooms, they too were alive with the sound of music – and a very different kind of music at that! For immediately the boys returned from school, rowdy activity resumed. The endless bouncing of footballs was enough to drive a cat mad; ferocious games of snooker sometimes led to cue poking, not to mention bowling from fast, hard balls; and worst of all, flashing TV and computer screens with loud audio back-up providing non-stop discord and a continuous droning din.

Sometimes it was just possible to hide away in the hall cupboard, or even to escape upstairs to the landing. But there too a cat could be pursued by pandemonium, and the ever-present threat of frantic vacuum cleaning. As for refuge in the bedrooms, that was a definite no! no! And *never* allowed. A sad fact that prompted Nimrod to recall apt lines from his favourite puss-cat poet:

Puss in the corner
Puss on the stairs
Puss in the basket
Puss on the chairs
Puss in the pantry
Puss in the shed
Puss may go everywhere
But NOT ON THE BED.*

[*Paul Gallico, *Honourable Cat* (Heineman, 1972), p.146).]

He had certainly been banned from beds, but Paul Gallico's ditty offered a cat more scope than the North Farm take-over seemed willing to provide. Yet trying hard to fall in with the new deal, Nimrod naturally used it to his own advantage. There were no Schnauzers after all, and only Cassidy – now, for some strange reason nicknamed 'Wezzle'! – competed for warmth by the Aga. And the smallest boy gave the cat siesta rights on a bright red bean bag, actually helping him mould really comfy positions for his elegant figure as part of the bargain.

Outside, no doubt because the newcomers showed little interest in gardening, Moles began to take over the lawns. In actual fact they came burrowing *under* the turf, carrying out an impertinent invasion Nimrod found so diverting that he used to spend long hours waiting for the next fresh mound of soil to rise before his very eyes! Nor did advancing years cramp his style as an alert predator,

accurate pouncing unearthing velvet prey on a number
of occasions. When engaged in mole watch too, he had
a way of avoiding threats from tabby rivals in the great
garden territory challenge. For he perfected a blinking
technique, finding it satisfactory and an easy procedure
to implement. So by closing his field of vision, he had the
satisfaction of knowing that any claimants were simply
out of sight, and therefore *need not be seen at all!* It was a
kind of cat chimera, a dream he'd imagined. But no such
fantasy kept Nimrod in dreamland when the time came
for action stations; and largely owing to Siamese vigilance,
the Moles were repelled.

Two other outside activities merit honourable mention.
First, the commitment of any cat to a family's social life is
unusual and deserving of biographical record. And as if
recalling his earlier rôle at those 'May Week' undergraduate
parties, Nimrod regularly graced barbecues with a Siamese
presence. The boys prized barbecues, and whether these
were held after games of soccer, rugger or cricket, or whether
they occurred as the climax of birthday parties, such occasions appeared in lights on North Farm's social calendar.
And celebrations that would normally have driven a puss
away, actually prompted Nimrod to act the host. Affability
itself, he met the guests; gave all visitors the once over;
flattered a favoured few with his best purring personality;
tucked into chicken nuggets and even sausage sizzle; and
once the festivities were over and the griddle cooled, did
sterling work clearing away and licking up.

Then too, no memoir can omit his concern for security.
Normally a canine rôle, guarding property has long been

a dog's principal duty. Indeed, if questioned, most house-holders keep such pets for two main reasons: company and security. But things are very different when it comes to cats. The company they afford their 'owners' is carefully qualified, no simple bargain, and a contract with uniquely feline terms attached. As for neighbourhood 'watch cats', have they ever figured? Well, briefly, with paw on cheek, and in his dotage, Nimrod often saw fit to warn the human underworld, making clear that North Farm was bugged, and that the red box prominently displayed outside indicated the installation of a genuine intruder alarm system. He would hide before Jenny went out; and then to his delight and her fury, leap on pressure pads and activate sensors until, summoned by bells, key holders raced to silence the signal and restore normality. The demands of daily life bear heavily on working mothers who have much to check before setting out on innumerable errands, and an evasive, sleepy puss was easily overlooked. In fact, it was almost a regular occurrence, just as his lofty appearance and smug sense of responsibility at the landing window confronted Jenny's hasty return as she swept up the drive to investigate. She was surely meant to hear catcalling: 'Only testing! No need to worry!' On one occasion too, when out of phase and in need of maintenance, non-stop ringing drove a distracted neighbour to climb up and muffle the bell box until the engineer could come to silence the alarm. The ladder was left in place, and when the Company eventually arrived to save the day, its technicians found a Siamese electrician already in place, seated securely on top of the box, ready and waiting to superintend the whole operation.

But such happenings were spirited highlights of Nimrod's last months, months otherwise largely given up to the solitary life, months of mounting loneliness weighing the cat down and even conveying a sense of abandonment. He could not have known that, once again, America had claimed his Obliger on a lecture tour; and somewhat frustrated, determined to seek out Peter for himself. Recalling full well the direction Peter took when taking his leave and setting out from the study for some unknown destination, he started to stray again. Familiar enough with Bill's house on the far side of the Green, he had at least the confidence to cross the road and explore a little further. A cautious survey of Clerk's Cottage gave valuable information about a King Charles Spaniel in residence there; and resting on Eileen Lambert's bench outside Widow's Cottage, he knew he must be nearer to his Obliger and there paused awhile in case Peter came back. He certainly experienced something of a thrill at the thought of solving his dilemma; but when distracted by tractors trailing up the lane to Manor Farm, could not find the courage to go on. So although new territories seemed well within paw range, his vision of Peter fast faded away into the pale world where the road meandered out of sight. Unwillingly or willingly, he therefore returned to North Farm. Disturbed by traffic, and unprepared for yet more noise, he longed for solitude and hurried back to familiar surroundings. He took what comfort he could from being by himself. For if a cat was really to make the most of nine lives, he had to cherish independence above all; and having learnt a great deal from his daylight sortie, he could surely contrive to hide away in the garden and sally forth again after dark?

And as far as will ever be known, that was what happened. But while Nimrod determined to avoid a night in – contriving instead to set out on his travels again – others conspired to steal an old car, and under cover of darkness try their hand at 'joy-riding'. Popular as a 'sport' to a group of local ne'er-do-wells, car theft, often followed by hit-and-run raiding, and car-burning to incinerate any evidence, was a growing menace. In the villages, pets were particularly vulnerable; and cats on the loose after dark actively persecuted by trips of trial and terror.

Sad to relate, that was Nimrod's fate. He must have been taken by surprise, for impaired with age, his hearing was less acute. And although rapidly approaching headlights must have helped him spot cars driven by maniacs with road-kill in mind, the nimble Siamese of yesteryear had slowed down. He could no longer judge distance with any accuracy, and vehicle speed was beyond him. How merciful then that he was killed outright – and for the record, he had at least lived the fullest of lives until the very moment he died.

Epilogue

I f Nimrod contributed to the prologue, any epilogue has to come from his Obliger. And granted the sense of loss all felt at North Farm, to pen such an obituary proved no easy task.

Peter certainly lost part of himself, for the passing of a greatly-loved pet can be as heart-rending as any death. It prompts mourning, and as if hearing loud 'miauuuus' from beyond the grave, memories of many a puss-cat prank poured in to underline the fact that a great character had left the planet. Where such a personality had gone mattered not at all; and there are fortunately no theologians to instruct the feline world. But once the little fur corpse had been laid to rest beneath his favourite hideaway at the far end of the paddock, the realization dawned that Nimrod's had been no empty existence.

To question the cat would surely confirm that fact. He had no regrets. And would doubtless point to his achievements as a hunter-gatherer, not to mention times of blissful revelling at the hands of those who obliged him. For however much he was always a law unto himself, Nimrod knew that he was greatly loved. His life had rarely been boring: and whether tracking down the Canterbury rat that threatened Jane's puppies; wreaking havoc in the 'Catswolds'; patrolling St Botolph's churchyard in Cambridge; supporting Downing's Dean of College; challenging that Barn Owl, and scattering the Starlings of Landbeach – a mischievous element of surprise was never far away.

Peter and Grace, Jenny and her boys, were angered and deeply distressed by the fatal road kill. Yet all knew that Nimrod and his kind demand and deserve the freedom to come and go as they please. Cats may enjoy being pampered, and like them all, Nimrod loved a fuss. He personified the friendly cat. Approaching with Siamese tail high, a chirrup and loud purr, he made clear that although his Obliger was first and foremost there to serve him, Peter could expect to be rewarded with high-quality feline affection. In almost twenty years service, and through regular sessions of grooming and care when the cat was off colour, he suffered hardly a scratch, so close was their bond.

The mere mention of his name thus prompts a pageant of nostalgia to come on parade. Disturbing images of battle contrast with hilarious scenes of laughter, and a rare ability to bounce back whatever the crisis. But the ultimate image to treasure is surely a profound memory of Nimrod walking in the garden in the cool of the day.

⋙⋘

Acknowledgements

It's quite a new experience for an historian to write an animal book; and readers have every right to question *how* and *why* a retired Cambridge don should turn from sixteenth-century studies to attempt the biography of a Siamese cat. Both queries demand answers: some are simple and straightforward enough; others more complex; but all have their place.

How the book came to be written is simply explained in terms of my lifelong interest in, and observation of, the natural world. Without animals, birds and plants, life on planet Earth not only lacks dimension and perspective, but denies humanity the inspiration needed for any kind of understanding, let alone progress. For without what little we know of the flora and fauna of our world, we are, all of us, sadly deprived; and in this twenty-first century we must surely learn to stop our thoughtless plunder of natural resources that have either to be treasured or lost for ever.

All of which leads to *why* and wherefore; and here the answer is more complex. First and foremost, these pages parade the life of an extraordinary feline and so have a peculiar fascination in themselves. Of that fact my Landbeach neighbour, retired architect John Burns, is clear. But that is not all, as context must count, if only to colour the narrative. And on generously agreeing to read the text, my colleague Christine Latham, MRCVS (currently lecturing at the University's Vet School), not only deserves *actio gratiarum* as a clinician for checking veterinary details, but also for commenting on the way Cambridge itself has changed in the last half century. For I have not attempted to update the story line, but rather made a determined bid to portray real puss-cat episodes as they actually happened in their period setting against the backdrop of a University life that no longer exists.

As a 'Research Student' it was my privilege to lodge with Mark and Sophie Pryor; and among my most treasured possessions I have an autographed copy of *Period Piece*, the fascinating insights of Sophie's mother, Gwen Raverat, into her Cambridge childhood. Nowadays, in large measure owing to media skills, social change is vividly recorded; and here may be seen something of a 'cat's eye view' of old Cambridge and my 'Domesday village', Landbeach, in the last quarter of the twentieth century.

Animal books invariably broaden human horizons, and although he had a passion for dogs, a definite debt to Sir Arthur and Lady Bryant must be acknowledged. For in 1960, that Olympian figure turned from Pepys, and countless excellent volumes of a *History of England* G M Trevelyan greatly admired, to write about a Jack Russell terrier. As he put it himself, this '…white, brown-capped, black, spotted, stuggy-tailed piece of fur and spirit… unexpectedly invaded and ruthlessly dominated' much of his existence. Undoubtedly the dog in his life – an animal whose story was partly played out in World War II and the London blitz – *Jimmy* provides a distinguished precedent. And

although all cat lovers – not to mention felines themselves!
– would object to pairing a mere mongrel with any Siamese,
Nimrod was the cat in my life. For me, he was the cat in
a million, and this *Memoir of Mischief and Mishap* sets out
the reason *why*.

Finally, kindly note that this is not just another cat
book. For there are cat books in plenty; they abound; and
interested readers with time to browse in second-hand
bookshops or 'on the web' can find a whole range of fascinating works. Some classics are sadly out of print, but
many remain available; and yet others are still widely read
and readily obtainable today.

Not long ago, that excellent BBC 4 programme 'Open
Book' broadcast a focus on felines as part of a post-Christmas
review of animal books. Presenter Mariella Frostrup discussed the latest dog and cat volumes, and, with Lynne
Truss, she despaired of run-of-the-mill publications, pleading that publishers take note and afford their public better cat [and dog!] books in future. So at the very moment
I was battling with my cat memoir, an appeal went out
over the air waves for studies that would at least try to
get into a cat's mind, as well, of course, as telling in good
prose a lively yarn from the feline point of view. And in a
book for adults – albeit a piece I have read to the delight
of my youngest grandson to whom these pages are dedicated – I have done what I can to set the record straight.
And the best is yet to come in so far as the line-drawings
of a long-standing friend and Cambridge colleague, the
accomplished artist Ian Levene, quite literally adorn the
text and afford him every accolade for making it so true

to life. Entrusted with the whole project, *Milton Contact* has likewise worked wonders; and the author's grateful thanks go to all involved, especially to Dr Chris Thomas for skills only the best in the business can provide.

PETER NEWMAN BROOKS

Landbeach,
Cambridgeshire